Pencil and Paper Games
for kids

¹M	O	²U	S	E
A		N		
³N	O	D		⁴B
		E		E
⁵H	O	R	S	E

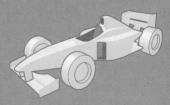

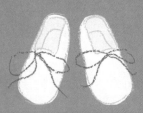

hamlyn

Pencil and Paper Games

for kids

Over 100 activities for 3–11 year olds

Jane Kemp and
Clare Walters

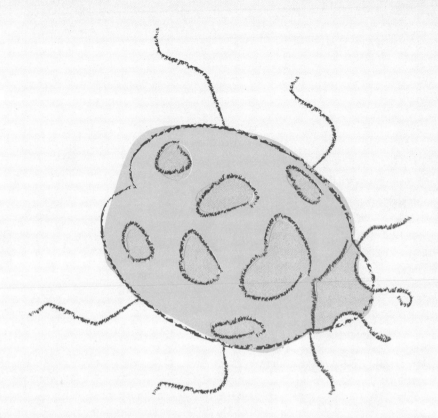

First published in Great Britain in 2006 by
Hamlyn, a division of Octopus Publishing Group Ltd
2–4 Heron Quays, London E14 4JP

Distributed in the United States and Canada by
Sterling Publishing Co., Inc., 387 Park Avenue South,
New York, NY 10016–8810

ISBN-13: 978-0-600-61483-8
ISBN-10: 0-600-61483-2

A CIP catalogue record for this book is available from
the British Library

Printed and bound in China

10 9 8 7 6 5 4 3 2 1

Contents

Introduction

A pencil, a piece of paper, and a little imagination – that is all you need to have great fun with your child. In an age when computers, expensive gadgets and electronic games are everywhere, it is refreshing to dip into a book packed with the easiest ideas at no great expense.

Here you will find games for all ages from three to eleven, with tips for beginners as well as ideas to make the games more challenging. In this way a favourite game for a young child can be adapted for play when she is older.

There are games that you and your child can play together, as well as those that work well for a group of children and some that can be played in teams. Some of the games will need preparation and a few need additional props. Games that involve a drawing of some kind are accompanied by an illustration.

Even the youngest of children loves to scribble and draw, and this is reflected in the simplest games in this collection. As your child grows older, the concepts of rules, playing fairly and taking turns become much clearer, and you will be able to expand the range of games that you can enjoy together.

For young children, you need to keep game times brief to allow for a shorter attention span. It is usually better to concentrate on introducing a child to a new idea rather than being too strict about how a game is played, so feel free to adapt the rules to suit your own child and family.

Check the index for games that are suitable for your child's age, but be flexible – sometimes children enjoy playing a game that is a little too easy, while others relish a harder challenge.

There are traditional games here, such as noughts and crosses and battleships, as well as a host of more unusual ones – just dip in and out to discover your child's personal favourites.

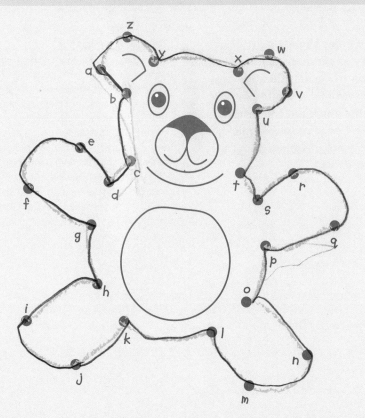

You will find that the games offer a unique chance to get you and your children enjoying activities together. They also challenge a child's intellect and help develop new ways of thinking and problem solving in a relaxed environment.

Games played in teams also help to foster cooperative play, which is good for developing social skills. Having younger and older children playing together on a team can be very helpful, as the older ones feel a sense of responsibility while the younger ones get the help they need.

The nature of the games – that they are played using just a pencil and a sheet of paper – means that they are easy to play at difficult moments, such as waiting at the doctor's surgery, whiling away the time on a long journey – even waiting for a meal to arrive in a restaurant.

Once you have taught your child how to play these games, they will be able to pass on the ideas to their friends. With luck, they might even choose to play a game instead of choosing to watch the television!

Chain drawings

Age range 5+
Number of players Up to four

All children enjoy the element of surprise in this game. By adding his own contribution to each of the drawings as they pass around the table – and in seeing how much fun the resulting pictures are – your child will quickly learn to be more imaginative in the figures he creates.

How to play

Each player has a sheet of paper and begins by drawing the head of a person, as far as the neck. The player folds the top of the sheet over to hide the head, leaving just the neck showing. He then passes his sheet on to the next person, who draws the body, including the arms, but not the hands. The paper is folded again, with just the waist left showing, and the papers are passed on. This time, each player draws the legs down to the knee. Finally, each player draws the lower legs and feet. The papers are passed on for the last time, and the players unfold their pictures for everyone to enjoy.

Tips for beginners

* Take fewer turns: for example, draw the head first, then the rest of the body.
* Make suggestions such as drawing the hair big and curly, adding a large belt or jewellery, or shoes with funny curly toes.
* Using different coloured pens for each body part makes it obvious where the different sections begin and end.

Variations

* Draw more complicated figures, such as wild beasts, or mythical animals.
* Have more players or take more turns: for example, the paper could be folded after the head, upper body, lower body, knees, ankles and feet.

What you will need A sheet of paper and a pencil, or coloured pen, for each player

Pencil walk

Age range 4+
Number of players One, with adult helper
What you will need A sheet of paper and
a pencil; coloured crayons or felt-tipped pens

A simple colouring exercise, this is great for younger children, who are just beginning to discover drawing for themselves. They will enjoy choosing and using different colours and many will rise to the challenge of keeping the colour within the outline of each shape.

How to play

Draw randomly all over a sheet of paper. Use any combination of loops, squiggles or straight lines, but do not take the pencil off the paper until the pattern is complete. Make sure the lines cross over each other to create a number of irregular shapes. Once this outline is finished, show your child how to colour in the shapes you have created.

Variations

* Older children can draw the random outline themselves.
* Draw a simple picture, such as a tree or teddy. 'Scribble' lightly over the image to disguise it, and mark a dot on each part of the scribble that contains your picture. Ask your child to find out what it is by colouring in all the dotted sections.

Tip for beginners

* Help your child to choose different colours when filling in the random shapes so that no two adjoining sections are the same colour.

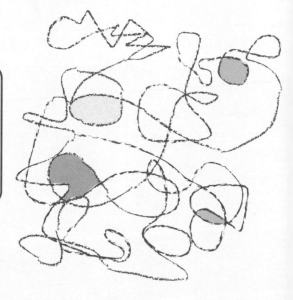

Mirror, mirror

Age range 6+
Number of players One, with adult helper
What you will need A sheet of paper and
a pencil; scissors, glue, an eraser (all optional)

This game will really test your child's
hand-to-eye coordination as well as her
observation skills. She has to 'read' a
drawing you give her in terms of outline,
scale and detail in order to match what
you have drawn. She will also need to
check your drawing constantly to make
sure she is on the right track.

Preparation
First, make a simple drawing of one half of a
symmetrical image, such as a face or a house with
windows on either side of the door. You may find
it easier to draw the whole picture, then cut it
down the centre and stick one half onto a fresh
sheet of paper, ready for the game. Or you could
draw the whole picture and erase half of it.

How to play
Give your child the half-completed drawing.
She has to complete the image by copying your
picture as accurately as possible, in 'mirror image',
on the opposite side of the paper.

Variations
* Try drawing funny opposites – for
  example, a man with a big bushy
  moustache on one side and a woman
  with long flowing hair on the other.
* Older children can add extra details to
  the finished picture, such as curtains in
  the windows of a house, or flowers by
  the door – as long as they appear on
  each half of the image.
* Your child can colour in the finished picture.

Tips for beginners
* Hold the half-completed image up to a
  real mirror, perpendicular to the surface,
  so that your child can get a clear idea of
  how the completed picture should look.
* Try the game with symmetrical letters
  (for example, H, M, O); or shapes such
  as squares, circles and diamonds.
* Use squared paper (or lightly draw
  squares onto the paper) to help your
  child with more complex images.

What a match!

Age range 5+
Number of players Two or more
What you will need A sheet of paper and a pencil for each player

Each child in a group has to follow the same set of verbal instructions in drawing a picture. It is fascinating to see just how different the finished drawings are from one another. This may be quite a challenge for your child, who has first to rely on his ability to visualize what is being described, and then to transfer that to paper.

How to play

Each player sits with his sheet of paper hidden from the other players. One player starts to draw a picture, describing it out loud as he draws, but without naming exactly what it is straight away. The other players then start to draw the same picture, following the description as carefully as possible. For example, the drawer might say: 'I am starting with a small circle, and drawing lots of little circles around the edge of it. It is a flower with petals. Now I am drawing its long stalk and a leaf on either side. There is a butterfly flying right next to it, and a big sun shining up in the sky. But there are two clouds – maybe it is going to rain.' As everyone finishes, all the players show their pictures, and see how closely they match each other – or how differently each person has interpreted the same description!

Tip for beginners

* Suggest very simple picture ideas at first, such as a square inside another, larger square; or a smiley face with long ears to make a rabbit.

Variation

* Older children can describe a more complicated scene to draw.

Age range 3+
Number of players One or more, with
adult helper
What you will need A sheet of paper and
a pencil

Odd one out

A good game from an early age, this
teaches your child to recognize basic
shapes and to make associations
between groups of similar objects.
The drawings can be as simple or as
complicated as you like, depending
on the age and ability of your child.

Preparation
Draw a row of images, where one is a misfit.
For example, draw a row of dolls with one teddy;
a row of smiley faces with one frowning; or a row
of trees with one flower.

How to play
Quite simply, your child has to look at the drawn
items and point to the odd one out.

Variations
* Spread the items around the page rather
  than in a straight line.
* 'Hide' the odd one out in a bigger picture.
  For example in an underwater scene, draw
  lots of identical little fish with a bigger one
  lurking behind some seaweed.
* Write out a sequence of numbers or
  letters from the alphabet, with a number
  or letter out of place. Ask your child to
  draw a line to lead the stray number or
  letter back to where it should be.
* Older children can create their own odd-
  one-out pictures.

Tip for beginners
* Point at each item saying its name – for
  example, 'rabbit, rabbit, rabbit...fish'.

Guess what I'm drawing

Age range 4+
Number of players One or more, with adult helper
What you will need A sheet of paper and a pencil for each player

In this game, your child has to guess what you are drawing. She cannot watch you, but has to listen carefully as you describe the picture as you draw. This can be fun for young children who will be excited to see how quickly they can make a right guess.

How to play
Start to draw a picture, describing it as you go. Be careful not to make it too obvious. Your child has to see how quickly she can identify what is in the picture. For example, 'It has got four legs and a tail. It likes eating grass and can jump over fences. Sometimes people like to ride them in races...' As soon as your child guesses, show her the picture, and she can help to finish it off.

Variations
* For an older child, make your descriptions less obvious. For example, a snake might be: 'likes to lie low...is a bit of a twister... likes to change its skin from time to time'.
* A group of children can take it in turns to draw and describe a picture.

Tip for beginners
* Describe readily identifiable things, such as a frog (is green, lives in a pond and can jump) or a ball (it is round, you can throw and catch it).

Buckle my shoe

Age range 4+
Number of players One, with adult helper
What you will need A sheet of paper and a pencil; coloured pencils

This game will make the most of your child's creative skills, encouraging her to think about using different patterns and colour schemes. It will also test her ability to copy accurately. You can even use the game to introduce the concept of left and right!

Preparation
Draw four pairs of identical, plain shoes or boots.

How to play
Give your child the paper on which you have drawn the eight shoes. Ask her to draw particular features on four of the shoes, making each one as different as possible. For example, the first could have funky laces; the second a large ribbon and buckle; the third could be stripy; and the fourth covered with spots. When she has finished the first four shoes, ask your child to draw exactly the same features onto the remaining shoes so that she makes four identical pairs.

Variations
* Have more pairs of shoes to begin with.
* Draw the shoes randomly over the paper and number each pair, so that the number ones, twos, and so on, must go together.

Tips for beginners
* Arrange the shoes with four down each side of the paper to make it easier to match them.
* Draw a line between each pair to join them up.

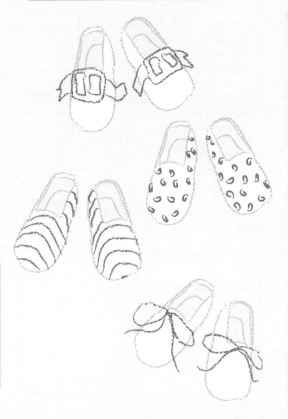

Gone fishing

Age range 5+
Number of players Two or more, with adult helper
What you will need A sheet of paper and a pencil; a felt-tipped pen for each player (optional)

In this game, your child has to identify which object is on the end of each tangled fishing line. This is a good exercise for hand-to-eye coordination skills and will also test your child's powers of concentration as he follows each line to its end.

Preparation

Draw four objects along the bottom of the paper – four different fish or other items such as a boot, a tin can, a key and a glove, for example. Along the top of the sheet, draw four fishermen with fishing rods. Now draw a fishing line coming from the first item, drawing randomly up the paper to meet with one of the fishermen at the top. Repeat with the remaining three items, crossing the fishing lines over each other to create a jumble.

How to play

Ask your child to trace along each of the tangled fishing lines, using either a finger or a felt-tipped pen, to discover which of the fishermen has caught each of the items.

Tips for beginners
* Use a different coloured felt-tipped pen to trace along each line.
* Keep the tangles uncomplicated so they are easy to follow.

Variations
* Draw up to ten items and fishermen, with a dense tangle of lines.
* Place the items randomly across the whole sheet of paper, rather than just along the bottom, before adding the fishing lines.
* Use the lines to match up other pairs, such as mother and baby (sheep and lamb, dog and puppy, hen and chick); or items that go together (knife and fork, cup and saucer, hammer and nail).

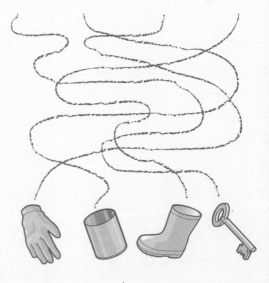

Age range 9+
Number of players Any even number over four, with adult helper
What you will need A sheet of paper and a pencil for each 'drawer' (see below); three additional sheets of paper

Picture clues

With just one minute allowed, one team member has to draw as many words as possible for his team-mates to guess. This is a real test of working under pressure: not only do the children have to think of the simplest drawing possible in a very quick time, but they also have to be able to draw it well enough for their team-mates to guess.

Variation
* Team members can take it in turn to do the drawing with each correct guess.

Tip for beginners
* Stick to words that are easy to draw.

Preparation
Cut each of the three additional sheets of paper into four to produce 12 game cards and write a single word on each of them, using a range of objects, activities and emotions. For example, you could have six objects (table, dog, hat, bus, door, horse); three activities (running, smiling, clapping); and three emotions (happy, cross, angry). Then turn the cards face down on a table.

How to play
The players divide into two teams of at least two people each, and choose one player who will be the 'drawer'. This player selects a face-down card from the table and has to make a drawing of the word you have written. His team-mates have to guess what the word is from his drawing: he is not allowed to say anything or make any gestures. Play continues for one minute, with the drawer taking another face-down card from the table with every correct guess from his team-mates. At the end of the minute all the correct guesses are counted up and scored for the drawer's team. Play swaps over to the other team, and the winning team is the one with the most points.

(Car)

(Happy)

(Running)

(Hat)

(Door)

Rhyme time

Age range 4+
Number of players One or more
What you will need A sheet of paper and a pencil

A simple rhyming game, this is one that children will love to play. A test of both word association and drawing skills, the first drawer will enjoy finding words that are a real challenge to find a rhyme for, and you can encourage the second drawer to come up with the funniest rhyme possible.

Tip for beginners

* If rhymes prove too difficult, draw pictures that are connected in some other way. For example, dog and basket, cat and mouse, bird and nest.

How to play

One player chooses a word such as dog, cat, mouse or bee, and draws a picture of it. The second player then has to find a word that rhymes with the first, and draw a suitable picture next to it. For example, if the first word was 'cat', the rhyming word could be 'mat' or 'hat'. Dog rhymes with log; mouse with house; bee with sea.

Variation

* Older children can make up silly rhyming sentences and draw these too, for example, 'there is a fish on a dish', or 'there is a frog lost in the fog'.

Age range 5+
Number of players One or more, with adult helper
What you will need A sheet of paper and a pencil

Missing links

See if your child can tell when something is missing from a picture. This is a good test of her visual skills, but also of her familiarity with everyday objects. She will enjoy completing the picture that you have managed not to get quite right!

Preparation
Draw a picture of a familiar object with a vital part left out. For example, draw a house without a front door, a horse without a tail, a bird without a beak, or a chair without one of its legs.

How to play
Show the picture to your child, asking her to look carefully to see what is missing. As soon as she has spotted it, she can draw it in.

Variations
* If more than one person is playing, they can take it in turns to draw the initial picture.
* Draw a picture where something is obviously wrong, such as bicycle with square wheels, a dog with two tails, or a fish with wings. Once your child has identified the problem, she can draw the whole picture again, correctly this time.

Tip for beginners
* Give verbal clues, or point to the picture where the missing part should be.

Pretty patterns

Age range 4+
Number of players One, with adult helper
What you will need A sheet of paper and
a pencil; coloured crayons (optional)

This game is a good test of your child's
mental skills – challenging his ability to
recognize a pattern emerging in a row of
figures or symbols, and to work out what
should come next. You can adapt the
game to test a wide range of skills: visual,
numerical, knowledge of the alphabet,
and so on.

Tip for beginners
* Use different colours for each shape
  as an extra visual clue to help your
  child recognize the emerging pattern.

Preparation
Draw a row of shapes that follow a basic
repeating pattern, leaving enough space at
the end of the row for your child to add to it.
For example, the pattern could be a row of
alternating squares and circles; or two circles
followed by a triangle; or two vertical lines
followed by two horizontal lines.

How to play
Ask your child to study the pattern carefully.
He then has to draw in the shapes he thinks are
missing to complete the row.

Variations
* Create more complex patterns. For
  example, choose three different shapes.
  Draw one of each to start with, followed
  by two of each, then three of each. See if
  your child works out that he now has to
  draw four of each.
* Use numbers or letters, for example, 1, 12,
  123, 1234, or alternate letters of the
  alphabet – a, c, e, g, and so on.
* Leave gaps to fill within the pattern, not
  just at the end.

Age range 5+
Number of players One or more, with adult helper
What you will need A sheet of paper and a pencil; a scarf (optional)

Shut eye

For this game, your child has to try drawing something with his eyes closed. The first few times he will find it very amusing to find that he makes quite a mess of things! With a bit of practice, however, it won't be long before he becomes quite skilled drawing blindfolded, and is able to move on to more complex images.

How to play
Tie a scarf gently over the eyes of your child (or he can simply close them), and suggest an easy subject to draw – a ball, a flower or a cup. When finished your child can look to see whether his drawing is reasonably accurate. Ask him to close his eyes again and try drawing something more complex like a fish, a cat or a shoe. Older children can attempt a whole scene – for example, a pond, a garden or a park.

Tip for beginners
* Let your child practise drawing the picture with his eyes open first.

Variations
* Ask your child to draw with his left hand if he is usually right-handed.
* Older children can try using their mouths, or even a foot to hold the pencil.

Spot the difference

Age range 3+
Number of players One, with adult helper

This is an old favourite with children of all ages. By studying two near-identical images for a couple of minutes, your child should be able to spot a number of differences between them – a great test of her observation skills.

Preparation

Draw two near-identical pictures, making one slightly different to the other in a number of ways. For example, draw a picture of a garden with a bird in one tree, but not in the other. Or you could draw one seaside scene missing a bucket, or with a fish jumping out of the sea.

How to play

Place the two pictures side by side in front of your child and ask her to identify what is different about one of them.

Tips for beginners

* Add the differences applying slightly more pressure with the pencil. This will produce darker lines and will make the differences easier to spot.
* Ring each difference as it is identified.
* Keep the picture simple, for example a flower with no leaves in one picture, and many in the second; or a face with eyes closed in one and open in the other.

Variations

* Show the pictures to your child one at a time, not together.
* Draw just one picture. After showing it to your child, hide it while you add one or more changes (or erase parts of the picture). Show it again – can she spot what has changed now?

What you will need A sheet of paper and
a pencil; an eraser (optional)

Word search

Age range 7+
Number of players One, with adult helper
What you will need A sheet of paper and a pencil (squared paper is helpful, but not essential); a felt-tipped pen

The aim of this game is to find a number of words hidden in a grid of letters. You can make the game more of a challenge by increasing the size of the grid and choosing more, or longer, words. Older children will enjoy making their own puzzles to swap with friends.

Preparation
Draw a 64-square grid on the sheet of paper, eight squares across by eight squares down. Choose a category, such as pets, and think of five words – for example, fish, dog, cat, rabbit and mouse. Write each of these words across or down your grid, with one letter in each square. Fill in the remaining squares with random letters to disguise where the correct words are hidden.

How to play
Give the grid to your child and explain that there are the names of five pets hidden among all the letters. Each time he finds a word, he has to draw around it in a brightly coloured pen. When all the words have been found he has finished.

I	Y	R	A	D	U	X	S
R	U	M	B	O	P	K	D
C	G	C	S	G	F	J	M
K	R	A	B	B	I	T	O
O	R	T	S	E	S	V	N
N	H	L	I	F	H	C	E
Q	T	A	M	O	U	S	E
H	U	O	B	T	P	Z	I

Variations
* Enter the words diagonally or running backwards in the grid.
* Overlap some of the letters of your chosen words.

Tips for beginners
* Draw simple picture clues around the edge of your grid to help your child identify the words he is looking for.
* Make a smaller grid with shorter words.
* Avoid words overlapping.

Age range 10+
Number of players Any number
What you will need A sheet of paper and a pencil for each player; an egg timer or a stopwatch

Letter sandwich

A group of children have a set time to think of as many words as they can beginning and ending with the same letter. This is a great test of your child's vocabulary and poses an extra challenge in having to find unusual or long words.

Tip for beginners
* Give clues to help new players. For example, 'a lion makes this noise'.

How to play
Each player has just five minutes to write down as many words as he can that begin and end with the same letter. Each player scores a point for every word, with a bonus point for any word that no one else has thought of. Allocate extra points for longer words, too.

Sample words
Taught

Taut

Rear

Roar

Sees

Sausages

Mum

Dad

Trumpet

Variations
* One player chooses one letter that all words have to begin and end with.
* Choose one letter for the beginning and a different letter for the end of the word. The winner is the first to think of a word that fits. For example, a word that begins with 'g' and ends with 'e' could be 'game'.
* Try to find words that are written the same backwards and forwards – for example, level and toot.

Build it up

Age range 8+
Number of players Any even number, split into two teams
What you will need A sheet of paper and a pencil for each team

Played with two teams, each player in a team takes her turn to write a word on a piece of paper that is passed from player to player. The idea is to complete a sentence as the words build up on the page. The challenge is for one team to complete a sentence before the other.

How to play
The first player from each team takes the pencil and writes down any word on the piece of paper. Then she hands the paper and pencil to the next player, who adds a second word. Each team member has a turn adding a word to the paper, where each word must be able to form part of a sentence on the page (although not necessarily in order). The winning team is the first to have completed a sentence.

Example of play
Five players might write their chosen words in the following order:

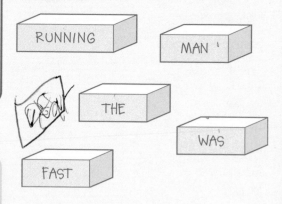

Together, the words can read:

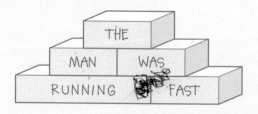

Tips for beginners
* Allow team members to discuss which words would be appropriate.
* Write words in grammatical order rather than randomly.

Variations
* Give each team the same starter word.
* With a small team, each player can take two turns to write a word.
* Do not allow any conferring between the team members.
* The final player's word must be the one to complete the sentence.

Zany verses

Age range 11
Number of players Any number
What you will need A sheet of paper and a pencil for each player

This is a poetic variation of He Said, She Said (see page 67), where some pretty strange tales are read out at the end of the game, much to the amusement of the players. Here the idea is the same, only the players have to write different verses of a poem.

Variation
* Use a limerick metre, which each player has to follow.

How to play
One player decides how many lines there will be in each verse of a poem, and whether or not they should rhyme. Then each player writes an opening verse, such as:

The night was dark and none
  could see
The ground where he was walking.
The snow fell thick but I could hear
An ugly sound of squawking.

Each player passes her paper on to the next player, folding the top over so that the next player cannot see what has been written. Each player might offer a verbal clue as to the subject of her poem to ensure that it makes some sense. For example, she might say 'It is about being in the woods at night'. Alternatively, the players might say nothing and simply see what happens next! They complete a second verse, fold the paper once more and pass it on. Four or five verses should be enough before unfolding the sheets of paper and reading out each silly poem in turn.

Tips for beginners
* Write just two lines at a time.
* Suggest possible rhymes.

Join up words

Age range 9+
Number of players Any number, with adult helper
What you will need A sheet of paper and a pencil for each player; an egg timer or a stopwatch

In this game, your child has to think of as many two-word combinations as he can that all start with the same word. It is a good test of his vocabulary. The game is played with a number of children, so each one is encouraged to think hard to write combinations that no one else will come up with.

Preparation
Choose a number of starter words that take on a new meaning when a second word is added. For example, you could have 'door', which can become 'door step', 'door stop', 'door knob', 'door handle' and 'door bell'.

How to play
Call out a starter word and give the children five minutes to add other words, so making as many new combinations as they can. Give an example to start them off. At the end of the time each child reads out his answers and scores one point for every word combination that no one else has thought of. The person with the most points wins.

Good starter words
Moon
Flag
Ice
Bread
Over
Fire
Train
Sea
Egg
Bed
Ring
Shoe

Tip for beginners
* Give some clues for the combinations, such as 'I am thinking of something that goes with rain and falls from the sky' (answer = raindrops).

Variations
* Try having the starter word at the end rather than the beginning of the combination. For example, 'boat' could become 'motor boat', 'sailing boat', 'rowing boat' and 'fishing boat'.
* Allow the starter word to be used at either the beginning or end of the combination. For example, 'paper' could become 'paper clip', 'paper bag', 'paper cut' or 'newspaper'.

Age range 7+
Number of players Any number
What you will need A sheet of paper
and a pencil for each player; an egg timer
or a stopwatch

Telegrams

Each child in this game has to make a
sentence, where each new word begins
with a specially chosen letter. It is amazing
to see how varied the resulting sentences
are, and just how versatile your child is
when it comes to playing with words.

How to play

Each person in the game takes a turn to call out
a letter, which every player writes down on the
left side of his sheet of paper. This continues until
the players have up to 15 letters written down in
the same order in which they were given. With
just one minute to play the game, each player
must write down a 'telegram' or 'sentence', using
the written-down letters — in the correct order —
to start each new word. For example, if the
letters were H, W, P, P, O, B, T, I, A, C, B, one
telegram could be: Hugh was painting pictures
of blue teapots in a cardboard box.

At the end of the minute, each player reads out
his version to the others and the best one wins.

Tips for beginners

* Use fewer letters for younger players —
  even three can make a sentence. For
  example, C, E, G could be cows eat grass.
* Have an adult choose all the letters, so
  that tricky ones are avoided, or suggest
  ways of starting the sentence. For
  example instead of Hugh was..., a
  sentence could start Hippos wear...

Variations

* Include the name of at least one person
  present in each telegram. (To do this, be
  sure to include initials in the list of letters.)
* Select a word that must be in everyone's
  sentence – for example, the T in the
  example on the right has to be teapot.
* The sentences must be on a particular
  theme. For example, sports or holidays.

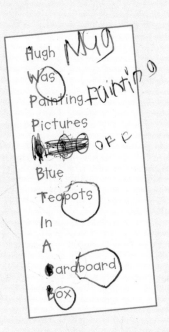

Sentence scramble

Age range 7+
Number of players One, with adult helper
What you will need A sheet of paper and a pencil

Here is a word game that tests your child's ability to make a sentence from a jumble of words. Older children will have fun making up their own confused sentences for their friends to attempt to unravel.

Tip for beginners
* Keep sentences very short, for example: The dog is wet; Fish like swimming; Tea is hot.

How to play
Think up a sentence and write it down on the sheet of paper, but mix up all of the words randomly. Hand the paper to your child and ask her to work out the right order for the words so that they make sense as a sentence.

Variations
* Make longer sentences.
* Spread the words randomly over the page, instead of in a straight line.
* Write each word in a different size, with some in upper case, some in lower.

Sample sentence

The red kite flew up in the air

might become

kite air flew the red up in The

Words within words

Age range 6+
Number of players Any number
What you will need A sheet of paper and a pencil for each player; an egg timer or stopwatch

This game has been a favourite among children for many years. Quite simply, it is a test of your child's vocabulary. One player in a group chooses a word and the other players in the group have to use its letters to make as many new words as they can. The challenge here, is to write down words that no one else will think of, because that is the only way to earn points.

How to play

An adult chooses a long starter word, such as 'nonsensical', and asks each of the other players to write the word at the top of her sheet of paper. Each player then has to write as many words as she can, using letters from within the starter word. She can use each letter only once.

At the end of five minutes, each player reads out her words in turn, with the other players crossing off any that appear on their own lists. At the end, each player counts up her score for the words she has left: four-letter words (and under) score one point; five-letter words score two points; six-letter words score three points, and so on. The player with the highest score is the winner of that round and chooses the next starter word.

Variations
* Use words with fewer vowels and more difficult consonants, such as 'xylophone'.
* Allow letters to be used more than once.
* Impose a shorter time limit.

Tips for beginners
* Use shorter starter words.
* Use words that feature plenty of vowels, such as 'elasticated'.
* Play the game in teams.

Nonsensical
No
Can
Clone
Con
Less
Slice
Lone
Ice
One
Loan
Nice

Triplet challenge

Age range 10+
Number of players Any number
What you will need A sheet of paper
and a pencil for each player; an egg timer
or stopwatch

Each player in this game has to think
of words that include the same three
letters, which makes it a good test of
both your child's vocabulary and his
ability to visualize words in his mind.
The same three letters can appear in
any order and any number of times in
the words your child writes down, which
adds to the challenge before him.

How to play

One player chooses any three letters, which each
player writes down at the top of his sheet of
paper. Within a five-minute time limit, the players
have to think of as many words as possible that
include all three of those letters. They can use
each letter as many times as they like, and a point
is scored for each word. For example, the letters
T, O and H can be used to make the words:

though
thorough
hot
touch
hoot

And the letters S, E and M can be used to make
the words:

message
smile
seam
messy
emeralds

Variations
* Use less common letters, such as I, K and J.
* Set a limit on how short the words can be
  – for example, no fewer than five letters.

Tips for beginners
* Include at least one vowel.
* Play the game with just two letters.

Letter leader

Age range 10+
Number of players Any number
What you will need A sheet of paper and a pencil for each player; an egg timer or stopwatch

When it comes to playing this game, your child will wish he was a walking dictionary! The idea is to take the same three letters and use them to start as many different words as possible. It sounds easy, but with one of the players deciding what the three starter letters should be, some rounds of this game may be challenging.

Variations
* Take each letter of the alphabet in turn when choosing the three starter letters (see below).
* See how many words each player can make within a one-minute time limit.
* Suggested starter letters are:
  AND, BAT, CAR, DOT, ENT, FIL, GRO, HOL, INC, JUG, KNI, LAM, MOD, NON, OFF, PUM, QUI, RUN, SIT, TRI, ULT, VIR, WEL, YEA.

Tip for beginners
* Play the game using just two starter letters instead of three.

How to play
One of the players suggests three letters, which each player writes down at the top of his sheet of paper. They then have five minutes to think of as many words as possible beginning with those three letters. For example, with the letters COM, a player may come up with the following:

comedy
come
compare
compass
communicate

With the three letters MON, a player might come up with:

mongrel
money
monk
monkey
monochrome

With the three letters SAL, a player might write down the following:

salt
saliva
saline
sallow
saloon

Players score a point for each word no other player has thought of and the winner is the player with the highest score.

Criss-cross words

Age range 7+
Number of players Up to four, with an adult helper
What you will need A sheet of paper (squared if possible) and a pencil

In this game, each child takes it in turn to write a new word in a grid. Younger children will be thrilled when they find a space that works for them, while older children will revel in thinking of words that gain them the maximum points.

Preparation
Draw a 100-square grid on the sheet of paper, ten across by ten down.

Variations
* Draw a larger grid for a longer game.
* Choose a theme that the words must fit in with, such as animals, space or school.
* Have a minimum length of word that can be used – say four, five or six letters.

Tips for beginners
* Use a smaller grid.
* Suggest a space where a word will fit.
* Suggest a word, and explain there is a space where it will fit.
* Allow a fresh start elsewhere on the grid if the players get stuck.

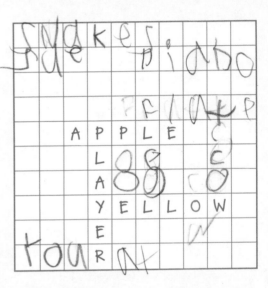

How to play
The first player writes a word in the grid, either vertically or horizontally, and up to six letters long. One point is scored for each vowel in the word (a, e, i, o, u) and two points for each of the other letters. The next player writes a new word in the grid, which must overlap the first word either horizontally or vertically. The remaining players take it in turns to add new words to the grid, until it is no longer possible to fit any more in. The last person to add a word wins a bonus five points. The winner is the player with the highest score.

Age range 3+
Number of players One, with adult helper
What you will need A sheet of paper and a pencil

Misfits

This game encourages your child to use her observational skills. Can she spot the odd one out?

Preparation
Write down the names of five objects, where four are related and one is not. Depending on the age of your child you can vary the game to make it more challenging.

How to play
Show the list of words to your child and ask her to identify which is the odd one out. Ask her to explain why. You could try the following lists:

Variations
* Have more objects in the list.
* Have two or three odd items.
* Make it odd for different reasons, for example, all the others begin with the same letter.

Tips for beginners
* Read out the list of words slowly.
* Draw a picture of each word.
* Put the odd word in the same place in the row each time.

Pig, cow, duck, sheep, crocodile
Plane, boat, car, train, drill
Sue, Mary, Kate, Vanessa, Robert
Trumpet, piano, saxophone, flute, kettle

Acronyms

Age range 10+
Number of players Any number
What you will need A sheet of paper and a pencil for each player

This game involves taking a word and using each letter in turn as the initial letter for a new word. The idea is to come up with a great name for a club or organization. Children will love to see who can invent the silliest club!

How to play

One player chooses a word of five or six letters, which each player writes in large letters down the left-hand side of her sheet of paper. For example:

A   or   S
L   M
E   A
R   R
T   T

Tip for beginners

* Use only three or four letters.

Each player then has to think of words starting with each of the letters that, when read out, sound as if they could be the name of a club or organization. For example:

American   Silly
Legal   Men's
Eagles   Arctic
Rally   Research
Team   Trust

Variation

* Create a grammatically correct sentence from the acronym. For example BECAUSE could become:

Big
Elephants
Can
Always
Understand
Small
Elephants

The winner is the first to finish. Alternatively, each player reads her own version in turn and the best one wins.

Age range 7+
Number of players Any number
What you will need A sheet of paper and a pencil for each player

All back to front

Children find this game of spelling words backwards very amusing. It fascinates them to hear how very familiar words can become so strange sounding. Encourage older children to move on to names other then their own – animals, places, cartoon characters – for example.

How to play

Each player writes her name down on a piece of paper. Next, she rewrites her name, this time spelling it backwards. The players take turns to read their 'new' names out to each other. Here are some examples:

Susan Davies

becomes

Nasus Seivad

Nicolas Peterson

becomes

Salocin Nosretep

Ben Martin

becomes

Neb Nitram

Variations

* Players with middle names can write them out backwards and say the whole new name with a flourish.
* Try writing down names using other familiar words, such as your middle name followed by a favourite pet's name. So instead of being Susan Davies, you might become Emily Fluffkins and Daniel Smith might be Gavin Smudge.
* Use your street name as a surname to see how it sounds. Make up exotic backgrounds and homes for your strange new namesakes.

Tip for beginners

* Skip letters that make awkward sounds when written backwards. For example 'Beth' can read 'Teb' instead of 'Hteb'.

Crossword creation

Age range 7+
Number of players One, with adult helper
What you will need A sheet of paper and a pencil

Test your child's wordplay skills by setting a simple crossword for him to complete. Older children can set crosswords for each other, which is quite a test, as they not only need to find a number of words that work together in a grid but also have to write clues for them.

Preparation
Draw a 25-square grid, five squares across by five squares down. Think of several words that can be set out across the grid so that they interlink (see illustration), but instead of writing the words in the grid, blank out any unused squares. Mark the first letter of each word – down and across – with a number. Now create a simple clue for each word and write the clues down the side of the grid, under two headings: 'across' and 'down'. Mark each clue with the number that corresponds to its place in the grid.

How to play
Your child has to solve each clue, in any order, and fill in the grid.

Example of play
Across
1   Small squeaky animal that likes cheese.
3   How you move your head to say yes.
5   Animal who says neigh and eats hay.

Down
1   A grown-up boy.
2   Opposite of over.
4   Makes honey.

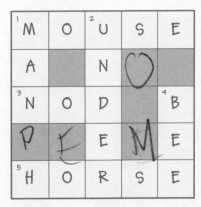

Tips for beginners
* Keep the words very simple, for example nouns only.
* Use fewer words.
* Draw a picture clue to go with each verbal clue.

Variations
* Make a bigger grid with 36, 64 or 100 squares, to allow for more challenging words.
* Use more cryptic clues, including anagrams. For example:
  PEELS back the covers for a good night's rest (SLEEP); or CORES mixed up – your points in the game (SCORE).

Age range 10+
Number of players Any number, with adult helper
What you will need A sheet of paper and a pencil for each player

Match the words

This is quite a challenging spelling game that can even catch out adults. The aim is to write down correctly two words that sound the same, but have different spellings. This will really appeal to children who enjoy playing with words.

Preparation
Write a list of five words that sound identical, but that have alternate meanings and are spelt differently. (See right for examples.)

How to play
Read two sentences to the children, telling them that each one contains a word that sounds the same but is spelt differently each time. Explain that the words also have different meanings. As the children listen, they have to write down the word, spelling it correctly in each case.

For example, if your word is 'which/witch' you might say 'The naughty girl took my pencil, which was better than hers'; followed by 'the witch flew through the air on her broomstick'. Treat each word pair the same way then check the answers. The child with the most correct spellings wins.

Word pairs	
Great	Grate
Blue	Blew
Too	Two
Toe	Tow
Sore	Saw
See	Sea
Weight	Wait
Shoe	Shoo
Knight	Night
For	Four
Would	Wood
Flour	Flower
Sole	Soul
Fir	Fur
Poor	Pour
Die	Dye
Buy	By

Tip for beginners
* Write down the alternative spellings for each word and let the children choose the one they think is correct.

Variations
* Spell one of the words in each pair and ask a child to invent a sentence using that word.
* See if the children can make more pairs.

Look inside

Age range 7+
Number of players One, with adult helper
What you will need A sheet of paper and
a pencil

This clever game will test not only
your child's spelling ability, but also her
observational skills as she has to search
for words that are hidden among the
other words in a sentence.

Preparation

Choose a theme – say animals, transport or toys
– then select a few words from the theme to hide
in a sentence. For example, from animals you
could choose 'cat', 'donkey', 'fish' and 'badger'.
Make up sentences, where each contains one of
your chosen words.

Sample sentences

The magic **at**las had a talking map.

In Lon**don key**s are kept on hooks.

A tin roof **is** hot in summer.

Oh no, that **bad ger**bil has nibbled
the wire again!

How to play

Write down the words you have hidden, for
example, the names of the four animals, then
show your child the sentences you have made up
and ask her if she can spot the words hidden
within them. Explain how she will need to look
between the words to find them, and show her a
sample sentence to get her on the right track.

Tip for beginners

* Keep both words and sentences short.

Variations

* Hide two words within one sentence.
* For an older child, try hiding a secret
  message within several sentences, such
  as a task that she has to carry out. For
  instance, if your secret message is 'Touch
  your nose', your sentences could be:
  He said it fel**t ouch**y!
  Lucky **our** food lasted out.
  There are **no se**ttlers here.

Age range 8+
Number of players Any number, with adult helper
What you will need A sheet of paper and a pencil for each player

Name race

Playing this game will demonstrate how versatile your child's vocabulary is. Playing with a number of children means that each benefits from the others' contributions, and they all build up their words over time.

How to play
Choose a category, such as small animals or garden flowers and ask the children to write down as many names as they can think of within that category in the space of five minutes. At the end of the five minutes ask each child to put down her pencil and read out her list. The child with the most words wins, and you can award extra points for unusual or imaginative answers.

Possible categories
Things that live in the sea
Names of towns
Languages
Flying creatures
Playground games
Toys
Board games
Things that have wheels
Nursery rhymes
Story books

Flying creatures
Bird
Wasp
Butterfly
Bat
Moth

Variations
* Ask the child with the most points from the previous game to choose the category for the next game.
* Read out a list of items and ask the children to guess what the category might be.

Tip for beginners
* Team up a younger child with an older one, who can write down the answers more easily.

Slithering snakes

Age range 4+
Number of players One, with adult helper
What you will need A sheet of paper and a pencil; coloured pencils (optional)

This is a simple counting game with a twist. Your child has to count the number of snakes you draw on a sheet of paper – but all the snakes are jumbled up. A good test of visual as well as numerical skills.

Preparation
Draw a pile of wiggly snakes on the sheet of paper (see illustration, below). The first one you draw will be the top one. Now draw one beneath – making sure you do not overlap any lines where the snakes cross. Continue to draw more snakes, always being careful to connect the lines correctly. Do not give any of the snakes eyes.

How to play
Ask your child to look closely at the pile of snakes and see if he can count how many there are all together. Challenge him further by seeing if he can also work out which snake is at the bottom of the pile and gradually work up to the one on top.

Tips for beginners
* Give the snakes eyes to make it easier to count them.
* Tell your child to colour in each snake as he counts it.

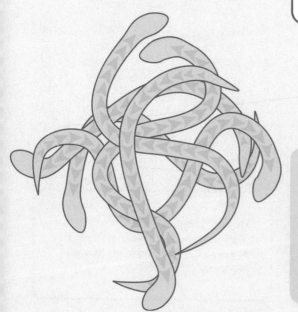

Variation
* Draw two eight-legged spiders and one seven-legged spider, with as many legs as possible crossing over each other. Ask your child if he can disentangle the spiders to find out which one has only seven legs.

Picture letter

Age range 6+
Number of players One, with adult helper
What you will need A sheet of paper and a pencil

Can your child read a letter that has been written half in words and half in pictures? Children love this game and will enjoy working out what your letter says. An older child can make up his own picture letter in reply to yours.

Preparation
Write a simple letter, replacing some of the words with pictures (see illustration, below).

How to play
See if your child can work out what the pictures mean, and thereby read the letter out loud.

Variation
* Split a word so that half is a picture, while the rest is made of letters.

Tips for beginners
* Read the main portion of the letter out to your child, leaving him to decipher the picture clues.
* Only replace nouns with pictures.

Dear Billy,

Please come to my .

You can play with my

 and see my .

We will have a

for tea and watch

. I hope you

can come.

♡ from Susan.

Lion and tiger

Age range 6+
Number of players One, with adult helper
What you will need A sheet of paper;
a pencil for each player; two coloured
pencils (optional)

Also known as 'boxes', this game is a well-known favourite, in which players take it in turns to try and form squares by joining dots on a grid. Older children can draw the grids themselves.

Preparation
Draw a 25-dot grid, five dots across by five dots down (see illustration, right).

How to play
Decide who is going to be the lion and who is going to be the tiger. Each player takes it in turns to join any two adjacent dots with a straight vertical or horizontal line, until one of them draws a line that completes a square. The person who forms the square puts her initial (L for Lion, T for Tiger) inside the 'box' and joins two dots somewhere else on the grid. If this line completes another box, she gets another turn. More squares are made as the game progresses and play continues until it is impossible to complete any more squares. The lion and the tiger count up how many squares they each have, and the winner is the one with the most.

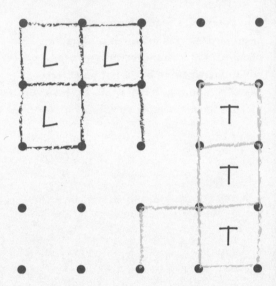

Variations
* More advanced players can use a larger-sized grid.
* Try speed play, which leaves no time to linger over your choice of line.

Tip for beginners
* Use a different coloured pencil for each player so that counting up the initials in the squares is easier.

Age range 6+
Number of players One, with adult helper
What you will need A sheet of paper
and a pencil; an eraser; two same-coloured
counters for each player (for example, two
blue and two yellow)

Round the bend

This is a simple game involving moving
counters on a grid. Younger children will
enjoy finding somewhere to move to, while
older children will love to see if they can
work out the perfect strategy for winning.

Preparation

In pencil, lightly draw a rectangle (landscape
format) with two diagonal lines joining the four
corners. Erase the top line, and mark a circle at
each of the four corners and at the point where
the diagonals intersect.

How to play

Place two blue counters on the top two corners,
and two green counters on the bottom two
corners. The first player moves one counter along
a line to the centre circle. The second player
moves her counter along a line and into the first
player's old space. The game continues like this
until one of the players can no longer move
either of her counters and is the loser.

Tip for beginners

* Suggest where your child should move if
  she finds the game difficult to start with.

Variation

* Two older children can play the game,
  either drawing the grid themselves, or
  asking an adult for help.

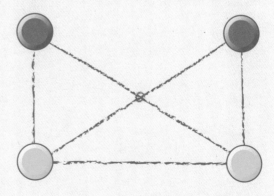

Streets ahead

Age range 7+
Number of players One, with adult helper
What you will need A sheet of paper and a pencil

The aim of this game is to see if your child can match a visual clue to a written one. You can make the game more fun by telling a story to help your child identify the different streets.

Preparation

Draw a very simple grid of a number of parallel roads, each with a feature or characteristic of its own – say a tall tree, a cat, a flowerbed, a cottage and a lamp post. Write a list of road names beneath the grid, in no particular order, but where each street name can be linked to one of your visual clues.

Examples of street names:

Tall Tree Avenue
Pussy Cat Walk
Posy Place
Cottage Close
Lamp Post Lane

How to play

Ask your child to write the correct name along each of the roads you have drawn, matching them up to the visual clues you have drawn.

Variation

* Make your map more complicated, adding crescents (Moon Crescent), wiggly roads (Snake Pass), roundabouts (Flowerbed Roundabout), and parks (Boat Lake Park).

Tip for beginners

* Write the road names in the order in which they appear on your map.

Age range 7+
Number of players One, with adult helper
What you will need A sheet of paper and a pencil; a damp teabag (optional); crayons (optional); coins (optional)

Treasure map

Children love games of hide and seek and this is no exception. You have to find your child's hidden treasure and having the upper hand in this game will encourage your child to be artful in avoiding a quick discovery.

Tips for beginners

* Draw the map for your child.
* Draw the treasure chest in one corner, helping your child to make crayon rubbings of real coins for the treasure.

Variation

* You can give the map an aged look by tearing the edges of the paper and rubbing it over with a damp teabag before you start. Make sure the paper is completely dry before your child starts to draw, otherwise it might tear.

How to play

Ask your child to draw the outline of a large, empty treasure island and offer suggestions of features that he might like to draw on his island. For example, he could draw a sandy cove; a slimy swamp; a waterfall; a dark forest; a bottomless lake; caves; cliffs; and mountains – appeal to his sense of adventure.

Once the island is complete, your child must choose one location to 'hide' his treasure – he should not tell you where it is. Taking the picture from your child, pretend to be a pirate seeking the treasure. Draw a dotted line as you move around the island, with your child saying 'hot', 'cold' or 'warm' each time you approach a new area. When you reach the right spot, he shouts 'Gold!' and you can mark the spot with an X.

Dice code

This game is similar to Words Within Words (see page 31), except that, here, the letters start out as numbers! This means your child has to be good at code breaking as well as at making up words under pressure.

Preparation

Write down all the letters of the alphabet on the extra sheet of paper and cut out each letter so that you have 26 individual squares. Add a small 'u' next to the 'q'. Place the vowels (A, E, I, O, U) in one bag and the consonants (B, C, D, F, and so on) in another.

How to play

Choose one person to be the 'caller'. The caller picks a letter from the vowels bag, say E, and calls out 'I is E'. The players write this down. Then the caller selects another vowel and calls out '2 is A'. The caller selects four consonants in the same way, until each player has a list of six numbers and their corresponding letters on her sheet of paper. For example:

1 = E
2 = A
3 = P
4 = R
5 = S
6 = T

Variations

* Play a second round using the same number code – the die will throw new combinations – or by selecting a new set of letters from the bags.
* Throw the die more times to get more letters and so make longer words.
* Allow each letter to be used more than once. From the example on the right you might also be able to make: steep, peep or state, for example.

What you will need A sheet of paper and a pencil for each player, plus an extra sheet; scissors; two bags; a die; an egg timer or stopwatch (optional)

The caller then throws the die and calls out the number it lands on. Everyone writes this down. The die is thrown five more times, until each player has six numbers on her sheet of paper. The players now have one minute to swap the numbers for letters and make as many words as they can, using each letter once only. For example: if the numbers were 3, 1, 2, 3, 5, 6 the letters would be P, E, A, P, S, T, which could be used to make the following words: pea, peas, peat, pat, sat, sea, tea, sap, tap, set, pet and so on.

At the end of the minute, each person reads out her list of words in turn, crossing off any word that someone else also has and scoring one point for every word left. The player with the most points wins.

3	1	2	3	5	6
P	E	A	P	S	T

Pea
Peas
Peat
Pat
Sat
Sea
Tea
Sap
Tap
Set
Pet

Tips for beginners
* Remove any difficult consonants from the bag (X, Z or Qu).
* Score a point for every word made, even if someone else has it.

Order, order!

Age range 7+
Number of players One, with adult helper
What you will need A sheet of paper and a pencil; scissors (optional)

Does your child know the seasons of the year and the days of the week? Test his knowledge by presenting words to him in the wrong order and seeing if he can put them right.

Preparation
Choose a set of words that always go in a familiar order, for example: the days of the week; the months of the year; the colours of the rainbow. Write the words on a piece of paper, but with the order all jumbled up.

Variation
* Write out a familiar nursery rhyme or favourite poem, jumbling the words and asking your child to unscramble them.

How to play
Ask your child to write a number next to each word, so indicating the right order for them to go in. For example:

Tuesday 2
Sunday 7
Wednesday 3
Monday 1
Friday 5
Saturday 6
Thursday 4

Alternatively, cut out each word in the list and see how quickly your child can lay them down in the correct order.

Tips for beginners
* Choose a very short list to mix up, such as the seasons, or who is tallest or oldest in your family.
* Mix up the names of familiar nursery rhyme or story characters. For example: Gingerbread Dumpty; Humpty Man; Little Red Simon; Simple Riding Hood.

Catch the thief

Age range 9+
Number of players One, with adult helper
What you will need A sheet of paper and a pencil

If your child does not know his left from his right already, this is a great way to teach him. In this game he has to follow a simple set of directions to help catch a thief.

Preparation
Copy the illustration to create a simple network of roads lined with blocks of flats. Mark a 'start' point somewhere in the drawing and give each block of flats a letter.

How to play
Explain to your child that a policeman is trying to catch a criminal who is hiding in one of the blocks of flats. Your child has to help the policeman by following your directions to the hideout. Write the location of the hideout on a piece of paper and turn it face down. Then ask your child to draw a route according to your instructions. For instance, 'Turn left and go along the road until you come to the first junction. Turn right and go past two turnings' and so on. When your child has arrived at the correct location, ask him to stop and turn over the piece of paper to check whether he is right.

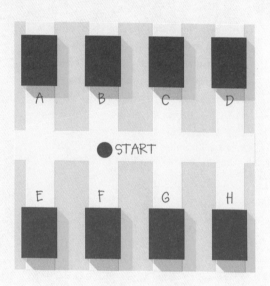

Tip for beginners
* Write a little 'r' on your child's right hand and an 'l' on his left hand to help him know which way to turn.

Variations
* Draw a more complicated map with road names and use these in your instructions.
* Instead of a policeman chasing a criminal, make it a squirrel looking for her stash of nuts, or two friends playing hide and seek.

Activity codes

Age range 9+
Number of players Any number, with adult helper
What you will need A sheet of paper and a pencil

This game involves giving your child a simple instruction, say, to scratch her nose. The problem is, that you give it to her in code. Once she's revealed the message she'll relish carrying out the task.

Preparation
Substitute a number for each letter of the alphabet, for example A=1, B=2 and so on, up to Z=26.

A = 1	J = 10	S = 19
B = 2	K = 11	T = 20
C = 3	L = 12	U = 21
D = 4	M = 13	V = 22
E = 5	N = 14	W = 23
F = 6	O = 15	X = 24
G = 7	P = 16	Y = 25
H = 8	Q = 17	Z = 26
I = 9	R = 18	

How to play
Write out a secret message in the number code and ask your child to crack the meaning by replacing numbers with letters again. Each child in a group could receive a different instruction, along the following lines:

Stand on one leg
Clap six times
Run up the stairs
Touch your toes
Curl into a ball
Jump three times

Tips for beginners
* Let your child keep the key to the code in front of her as she works it out.
* Get her to decipher simple, single action words such as jump, shake, hop, skip, run or wobble.

Variations
* Make your code more difficult by counting three letters along, so A=D, B=E, C=F and so on.
* If you have a word processor or a computer, you can transform a whole list of code sentences by changing the typeface into one that uses symbols (for example, Zapf Dingbats).
* Make a code by removing all the vowels from the words in each sentence and run the words together. For example: TOUCH YOUR KNEES becomes TCHYRKNS.

Spot the cities

Age range 10+
Number of players One, with adult helper
What you will need A sheet of tracing paper and a pencil; an atlas

In this simple memory game, your child has to see how many city names she can remember having looked at a map. This is a great way to learn the basic whereabouts of major cities in your country and others.

How to play

Give your child a simple map of your country and ask her to trace the outline carefully. Help her to mark in the major cities with dots, repeating the name of each one as you do so. Show her the simple map again and let her look at it for a while. Close the atlas and see how many of the city names she can fill in on the outline she has drawn from memory.

Variations

* Add in a few other details, such as rivers or mountain ranges.
* Try tracing the outlines of other countries and filling in the capital cities.
* Make up a country of your own for your child to trace, inventing fun place names for her to memorize.

Tip for beginners

* Write the first two letters of each city's name beside each dot.

Nine men's morris

Age range 10+
Number of players Two
What you will need A sheet of paper and a pencil; 18 counters (nine each of two colours)

Also known as 'Mill' in the United States, this board game has always been popular. By placing and moving his counters around the board, each player aims to remove his opponent's counters from the game. If he manages to reduce his opponent to two men, or to corner him so that he cannot make a move, a player has won.

Preparation
Copy the illustration below to create your own playing board.

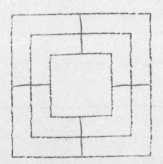

How to play
Each player has nine counters, or men, and takes turns to place them on the board one at a time. He can place the counter either on a corner or where two lines intersect. As soon as a player has three men in a line (known as a 'mill'), he can remove one of his opponent's men from the board. That man is then out of the game, or 'dead'.

Once both players have all of their counters on the board they continue play by moving them around the board. With each move, however, a player must move his counter to an adjacent point in a line. If a player makes a mill he removes an opponent's piece from the board. The game ends when one player has just two counters remaining, or is unable to move a piece on the board. He is the loser.

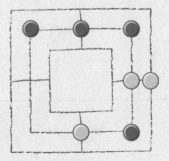

Variation
* When one player is down to three men (one man away from losing), let him jump over his own pieces to get a new position.

Tip for beginners
* Mark each of the 24 positions on the board so that each player can easily see the available spaces for his counters.

Safe cracker

Age range 11
Number of players Two
What you will need A sheet of paper and a pencil; felt-tipped pens (optional)

There is an element of chance to this game, in which one player has to guess his opponent's secret four-digit code. There is a call for some clever deduction too, however, which makes the game a real challenge.

Variations

* Play simultaneously on separate sheets of paper, taking turns to have a go.
* Play this game with different coloured dots instead of numbers.

Preparation

Draw a 40-square grid, ten down by four across.

How to play

The first player secretly writes a four-digit number on a piece of paper, using any figures from 1 to 8. The second player has to guess what those figures are, and writes his guess in the first row of the grid. The first player now marks the guess with a star for a correct number in the right place; a tick for a correct number in the wrong place; and an x for a wrong number.

The second player continues to guess the code, using the information from his previous attempts to revise his selection of numbers. If he gets the code right before reaching the top of the grid, he has cracked the code and is the winner.

Tip for beginners

* Play with fewer numbers.

4^*	1^*	5^*	7^*
4^*	$7^✓$	$1^✓$	$5^✓$
3^X	$4^✓$	$7^✓$	$1^✓$
2^X	6^X	9^X	$4^✓$

Spy letters

Age range 11
Number of players Two, with adult helper
What you will need A sheet of paper for each player, two sheets of squared paper and a pencil for each player; sharp scissors

This game will appeal to the spy master in your child. The aim of the game is to break a coded message. It sounds simple, and it would be if your child did not have to find the message first!

Preparation

Each player needs to think of a short message and write it down on a piece of paper. For example, one player may come up with MEET ME IN THE PARK. Agree on a code, say, moving each letter of the alphabet one to the right, so that A becomes B, B becomes C and so on. Each player now needs to convert her message using the code. The message above would now read: NFFU NF JO UIF QBSL.

Each player writes her coded message on her first sheet of squared paper. She has to write one letter in each square and can leave a random number of blank squares between the words. Laying the second sheet of squared paper over the first, the player marks the squares where the letters show through. If the player cuts these squares out carefully, and lays the second piece over the first again, she should now be able to read her coded message through the holes. Returning to the first sheet of squared paper, the player now fills in the blank squares between the words of her coded message with random letters, thereby 'hiding' her message.

How to play

The children swap both their sheets of paper. The race is now on for each player to work out her opponent's message. She lays the 'decoder' sheet – the one with the squares cut out of it – over the cryptic message. This reveals the coded message and the player then uses the agreed code to unscramble the secret message.

Tip for beginners

* Help your child when it comes to positioning the words and cutting out.

Variation

* Group the letters together in sets of four, with spaces between. This will make the decoded message harder to read.

Age range 10+
Number of players Any number, with
adult helper
What you will need A sheet of paper and
a pencil for each player; a ruler for each
player; coloured pencils (optional); an egg
timer or stopwatch (optional)

Busy hexagon

This game is an incredible test of your
child's visual skills. She has to count the
number of triangles hiding in a simple
hexagon. Every time she thinks she has
counted them all, she will spot another
one, and another, and...

Tip for beginners
* Use different coloured pencils to outline
  the various-sized triangles to make it
  easier to count them.

Preparation
Draw a large hexagon for each of the players.
Instruct them to use a ruler to draw a line from
each point of the hexagon to the three opposite
points on the shape (see illustration, below).

How to play
Each player has to count up how many complete
triangles there are within the hexagon. The
winner is the player who finds the most. (See
page 124 for the solution.)

Variation
* Set a time limit for how long players have
  to come up with their answer.

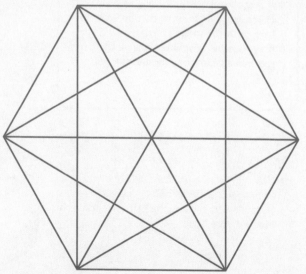

It's a bullseye!

Age range 4+
Number of players Any number, with adult helper

This fun target game does not require too much skill – any counter that lands on the target scores at least one point. Your child will need to hone his throwing skills to score the bull's eye, though.

Preparation
Make a large piece of paper by sticking together the four sheets. Draw five concentric circles approximately 7 cm (2½ in) apart. This is your 'target'. Write a figure 5 in the middle circle (the 'bull's eye'), a 4 in the next circle, a 3 in the next, and so on.

How to play
Lay the paper on a tabletop and give each player five counters. Standing behind a marker, each player takes it in turn to throw his five counters onto the target. When all five have been thrown the player checks the areas in which his counters have landed and writes down his total score. If a counter lands on a line between two circles, the lower score is chosen. At the end of the game, the person with the highest score is the winner.

Tips for beginners
* Adjust the marker according to your child's age and height so that he does not have to throw so far.
* If a young child's counter falls on the floor, give him an extra one for another go.

Variation
* Make the game more competitive by standing further away, adding more circles, or disallowing any counters that land on a line or on the floor.

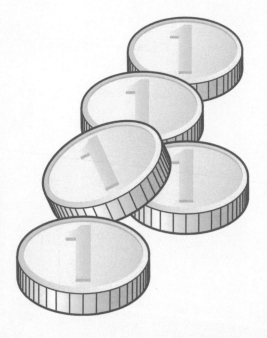

What you will need Four large sheets
of paper and a pencil; a bag of counters or
small coins

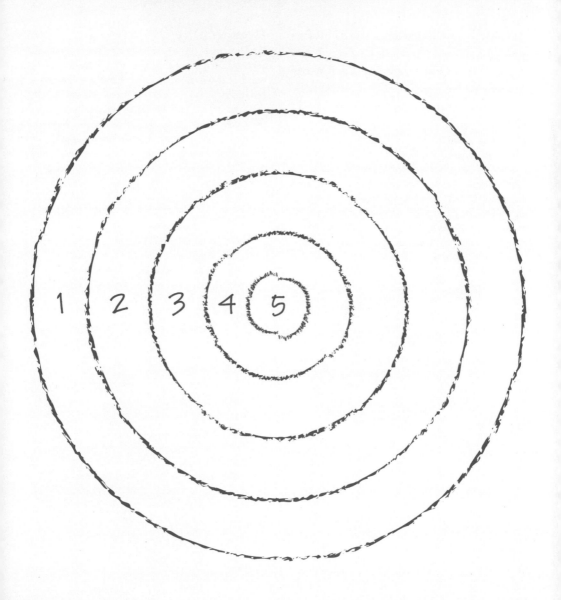

Lose your letters

Age range 5+
Number of players Any number, with adult helper
What you will need A sheet of paper and a pencil for each player; an extra sheet of paper; scissors; opaque bag

This game requires a keen eye as players cross off letters in a five-letter word as you pull them out of the bag. Each player has a different word, and the pressure is on to finish first.

Preparation
Write down the letters of the alphabet on the extra sheet of paper and cut each out so that you have 26 individual squares. Clearly write out a few five-letter words at the top of separate sheets of paper, one for each player. Useful words could include: house, stage, train, magic, watch, brush, woman, and party. Make sure no words feature the same letter more than once.

How to play
Put the cut-up letters into an opaque bag and give each player a piece of paper with a five-letter word at the top. Pick a letter from the bag and call it out. If anyone has that letter in their word, they can cross it off. For example, if you call out the letter 'N' and one player has the word plane, the player could cross out the fourth letter of her word. Shake the bag of letters and choose a new one. The first player to cross off all of her letters is the winner.

Tips for beginners
* Make sure the letters in the bag and in the words are all lower case and clearly separated so they are easy to recognize.
* Start with a three or four-letter word.

Variations
* Choose words in which a letter is repeated – 'river'; 'treat'; 'small', for example – and return each letter to the bag after it is called out.
* For older players, use longer words or give them two or three words to do at once.
* Play the game with numbers from 1 to 20 instead of letters, and have a row of five numbers for each player to cross off.

What's in the picture?

Age range 5+
Number of players Any number, with adult helper
What you will need A sheet of paper and a pencil for each player, some magazines, books or postcards; an egg timer or a stopwatch

By asking your child a number of questions about a picture that she has looked at, but which is now hidden, you can use this game to test your child's observation and memory skills.

Preparation
Choose a large detailed coloured picture from a magazine or book, or find some picture postcards. Think of a number of questions to ask the children in order to test their skills of observation and memory.

How to play
Allow a group of children to have a good look at the picture for one minute. Then remove it and ask a number of questions about the picture. For instance, if you showed them a picture of a seaside scene, you could ask if there were any boats in the picture and if so how many, or any sandcastles on the beach, or a café nearby, or anyone playing with a ball. Each player has to write her own answers on a sheet of paper.

Variations
* Play in pairs, with one player asking the questions and the other player writing the answers.
* Try an abstract version of the game by drawing a page of different coloured shapes and asking related questions. For example, 'Was the circle blue or orange?', 'How many squares were there?'.

If children of mixed ages are playing, ask individual questions – but keep a note of what you have asked each person so you can give them the right answers at the end of the game. When you have asked as many questions as you can, show the children the picture again and go through all the answers, scoring a mark for each correct one. The child with the highest score wins.

Tips for beginners
* Gauge the level of detail carefully for each age group.
* Choose a picture that you know will interest your child.
* Children as young as three can enjoy this game, but their answers will need to be spoken rather than written.

What's that word?

Age range 5+
Number of players Four or more
What you will need A sheet of paper and a pencil for each team; an egg timer or stopwatch

This is a simple word game in which one team player has to describe words to his team-mates. The more words they guess correctly, the more points they score. The challenge is in being accurate, because the children are playing against the clock.

Variation
∗ For advanced players, try more difficult words, including verbs (washing, ironing, jumping) and abstract concepts (art, science or colour).

How to play
The players need to group in two teams. The players in the first team think of five words from a particular category, such as buildings (church, house, village hall, school and police station), household objects, nature and so on. One player writes the words on a sheet of paper and passes the paper to a member of the second team. This player tells his team the theme, then describes each of the words in turn, without using any of the words themselves. For example, he might describe 'church' by saying 'this is a building where people go to pray'. His team members have to guess as many words as they can within a minute, scoring one point for each correct answer. Then it is their turn to supply a list of words for the other team to guess. When each team has had five turns, the points are counted up to find the overall winners.

Tips for beginners
∗ Stick to nouns in the word lists.
∗ Allow more time for guessing.
∗ Allow actions in the description as well as words.

Age range 5+
Number of players Two or more
What you will need A sheet of paper and a pencil for each player; an extra sheet of paper; a die

Beetle

This is a really great game, and one that children of all ages can play at the same time. Each has to draw a beetle, with every body part determined by the throw of a die.

How to play
Decide on which number on the die should correspond to which part of the beetle's body and write the key down on the extra sheet of paper. For example:

1 = body
2 = head
3 = tail
4 = eyes (two)
5 = feelers (two)
6 = legs (six)

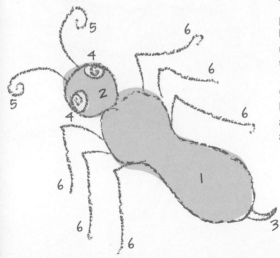

Variations
* Try the game with other creatures such as a spider, ladybird or butterfly.
* Play with two dice and draw two beetles at the same time.

Tip for beginners
* Start with the body and head already in place and let your child add the extra parts straight away.

The players take it in turns to throw the die. Each player has to throw a 1 to draw the body of the beetle first. He can then add legs and the tail, but must throw a 2 (for the head) before he can add the eyes and the feelers.

Once a body part has been drawn, the player has to miss a turn if he throws the same number again. The first person to complete his beetle with all 13 parts shouts: 'Beetle!' and is the winner.

Kim's game

Age range 8+
Number of players Any number, with adult helper

The idea here is that you place a tray of small objects before a group of children, who have a set time limit to try and commit each item to memory. Success lies to some extent on being able to identify the objects in the first place.

Preparation
Collect around ten small objects and lay them out on a tray. Good items to choose include: pencil, pen, sharpener, hair slide, teaspoon, paper clip, notebook, roll of sticky tape, bottle top, toy car, building brick, coin, wooden spoon, and so on.

How to play
The players sit in a circle around the tray, which should be covered with a tea towel to start with. Explain that once you remove the tea towel the players have one minute to remember as many items as they can before you cover it over again.

Once the minute is up and the tea towel is back over the tray, each player has to write down the names of as many things as she can recall. After five minutes, declare the game finished and uncover the tray. Hold up each item one at a time, saying its name. Each player can put a tick beside every word she has written correctly. The one with the most ticks wins.

Tips for beginners
* Put fewer items on the tray.
* Choose larger items that are more memorable, for example, a doll rather than a paperclip.

What you will need A sheet of paper and a pencil for each player; a tray with plenty of small items; a tea towel; an egg timer or stopwatch

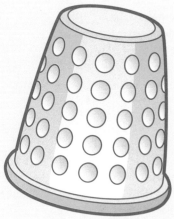

Variations

* Once everyone has looked at the tray, take one item away and see who is the first to spot which item has gone missing.
* Put a small number of items in a box instead and pass it around, allowing everyone one quick glance inside.
* Try a blindfolded version of the game whereby you pass around five or so items for each person to feel and remember. These items should be easily identifiable by touch, such as a hairbrush, comb, pine cone or feather.
* When it comes to marking the written answers, players can pass their sheets of paper to their left, so that each player marks another's results.

Sprouts

Age range 6+
Number of players Two
What you will need A sheet of paper; a pencil for each player; coloured pencils (optional)

In this game, all your child has to do is draw a line between two dots each time his turn comes round. The rules of play make this simple game quite a challenge, however, and victory quite often takes both players by surprise.

Variation
∗ Draw more starting dots for a longer game.

How to play
To start the game, draw two dots at random on the sheet of paper. The first player either draws a line to connect the dots or a line that starts and ends on the same dot (see illustration, below). The player then draws a new dot on that line. Play passes to the next player, with each player taking his turn to draw a line and add a new dot. The players must follow the rules below when adding lines and new dots and, eventually, it will become impossible for play to continue. The last person to add a dot is the winner.

Tip for beginners
∗ Use different coloured pencils for each individual player.

Rules of play
1. No dot can have more than three lines coming out of it.
2. A line cannot cross itself or another line.
3. A new line cannot go through a dot.

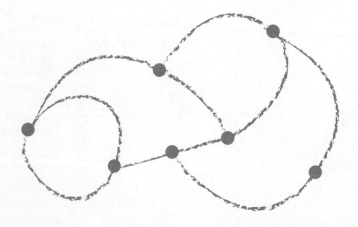

He said, she said

Age range 7+
Number of players Any number
What you will need A sheet of paper and a pencil for each player

This game is 'consequences' in its purest form. Each child takes it in turn to write the key facts in what happens when a boy meets a girl. Children love the element of secrecy here, and can barely wait to read out the silly stories at the end.

Tip for beginners
∗ Have a list of boys' and girls' names, locations, and so on, to choose from.

Variations
∗ Choose celebrity or pop star names for your boys and girls.
∗ Add more detail, such as 'he was wearing' and 'she was wearing' or a time of day, name of town or a country.

How to play
Each player takes a blank sheet of paper and writes a boy's name at the top. The player then folds the top of the paper over so that no one else can see the name. When everyone is ready the sheets of paper are passed to the left. Each player now writes down a girl's name and folds the paper over once more. The papers are again passed to the left and this time a location is added. Play continues by writing a short sentence a boy might say, followed a short sentence a girl might say, and finally a consequence. Players continue to pass the sheets of paper each time something new is written.

When all the papers have been passed to the left for the last time each player takes a turn to read out his 'story'. For instance one might read: Jim met Nancy on a ferris wheel. He said: 'I like chips'. She said: 'You're great!' And the consequence was: They rode off on a donkey into the sunset.

Treasure muddle

Age range 8+
Number of players Any number working in pairs, with adult helper
What you will need A sheet of paper and a pencil for each pair of children; an extra sheet of paper; scissors; some treasure

This game will appeal to all children who like playing with words – and finding treasure! Each hiding place has a scrambled clue, which the children have to work out before moving on to the next. It is a good idea to have treasure that can be shared among all players.

Tips for beginners
* Pair an adult and child together.
* Use hiding places that have shorter names to muddle up – for example, bath or bed.

Preparation
Choose ten hiding places around the house – for example, dining table, umbrella stand, kitchen sink, and so on. Write down the name of each hiding place, but muddle up the letters in each case so that you have clues that read something like ginnid balet (dining table), ballerum dants (umbrella stand) and hitenck kins (kitchen sink). Space the clues out over your sheet of paper so that you can cut them out easily. Choose one hiding place for the treasure, and leave a clue in each of the remaining nine hiding places.

How to play
Give each pair of children the first clue. They must unscramble the words to find the first hiding place, where the next clue is waiting. Each pair works through the clues – writing the next muddled word on their sheet of paper and leaving the original clue exactly as they found it – until the treasure is discovered in the final hiding place.

Variation
* Extend the game by having a short riddle to answer at each hiding place. For example, 'My first is in cup, my second is in jam, my third is in grit – can you guess me?'. The answer 'cat' could indicate that the next clue is in the cat basket.

BALLERUM DANTS

Football fun

Age range 9+
Number of players Two
What you will need A sheet of paper and a pencil; a coloured pencil for each player

This is a great game for rainy days that will appeal to your child's competitive nature. The skill is in moving forward without giving the opponent the chance to 'bounce' the ball for an extra turn.

Variation
* Draw a bigger grid for a longer game.

Tip for beginners
* Explain the benefits of 'bouncing' moves.

Preparation
Draw an 80-square grid – ten across by eight down. This is your football pitch. Add two squares at each short end for the goals (see illustration, below). Mark a point in the centre of the pitch. This is your ball.

How to play
Using a different coloured pencil each, the players take it in turns to move the ball from the centre of the pitch to their goal. A player can cross one square at a time – horizontally, vertically or diagonally – drawing a line to indicate her move. Her opponent does the same, but moves in the opposite direction. Play continues with players zig-zagging across the pitch until one of them reaches her goal. During play, if the ball touches either the sides of the pitch or a line that has been drawn already, it 'bounces' off and that player has another go.

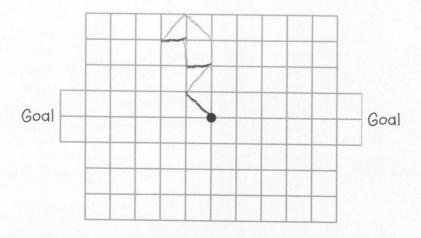

Goal   Goal

Explain the meaning

Age range II
Number of players Any even number

This is a great exercise for testing your child's verbal dexterity – can he think up a convincing 'wrong' definition for a tricky word? Half the fun in this game is in trying to bluff his opponents into believing him.

Preparation

Before playing the game, select ten or more words from a large dictionary, choosing words that you think the players will not recognize. Cut the extra sheet of paper into ten strips and write a word on each, with the definition beside it.

How to play

With the players working in two teams, each one takes a slip of paper with a word on and has to invent two incorrect definitions for the word. After five minutes, the teams take it in turns to read out the three definitions of their word to the opposite team, which tries to guess which is correct. In each case, a team member should write the word out in large letters for the opposition to see.

Variations

* Use people's jobs instead of random words. For example, a steeplejack (someone who repairs steeples and chimneys), a topiarist (someone who cuts hedges) or a stevedore (someone who loads and unloads shipping vessels).
* Instead of guessing the meaning of a word, try guessing what a word is from three correct descriptions. For example. 'This is something you'd use to eat with', 'This object has tines', and 'You wouldn't drink soup with this'. The answer here is 'fork'.

Example:
What is a quadruped?
A. An animal with four legs?
B. A bike for riding over rough countryside?
C. A country dance?
Answer: A

What you will need Five sheets of paper and a pencil for each team; an extra sheet of paper; scissors; a dictionary

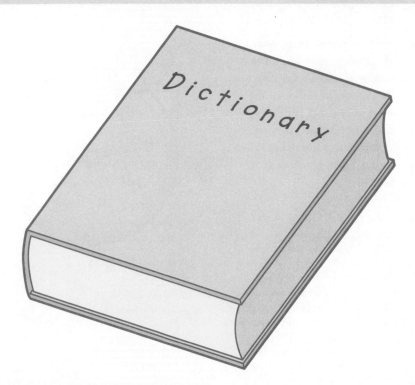

Example of play
If the chosen word was beeves, the three descriptions could be: 'another word for cattle or oxen' (correct), 'an unusual sort of hive made by wild bees' (false), and 'a nickname for people who know a lot, like Jeeves' (false). Of course, each definition can be much longer than this, and elaborated upon as much as the players like. If the guessing team gets the answer right, they get one point. Play then passes to the other team, and the team with the highest score wins the game.

Tips for beginners
* Explain to players that the game works best if the wrong definitions sound as convincing as the correct ones, and so a straight face is essential.
* Make sure that everyone is involved. If there are several people playing you could choose three different people to read out the definitions.

Categories

Age range 8+
Number of players Any number
What you will need A sheet of paper and a pencil for each player; an egg timer or stopwatch

This is a word game that tests your child's ability to think of words of the same type – animal names, for example – starting with a range of different letters. Not only that, but she has to play against both time and other players. There are no points for two players writing down the same word, so this game calls for great concentration.

How to play

One player – the 'caller' – chooses a five-letter starter word, such as 'plane', 'spade' or 'diver'. Each of the remaining players then writes that word across the top of her sheet of paper, with the letters well spaced out, heading each of five columns. The caller then announces a category, such as girls' names. The other players have two minutes in which to write down a girl's name beginning with each letter of the starter word. For example, if the starter word is 'plane', a player might choose the following girls' names:

P L A N E
Polly Lucy Anne Naomi Emma

Each name wins a point – but only if no one else has used the same one. The player with the most points is the winner of that round. The caller chooses a new category for the next round, say, boys' names, foods, animals or household objects, and so the game continues.

Variations

* Choose a starter word with unusual letters, such as 'quick' or 'amaze'.
* Choose longer starter words such as 'tickle' or 'ghostly'.
* Choose more difficult categories, such as countries, flowers, colours or gemstones.

Tips for beginners

* Use a shorter starter word, such as 'mat' or 'hen'.
* Keep the categories easy.
* Allow more time.

Age range 9+
Number of players Any number
What you will need A sheet of paper and
a pencil for each player

Story circle

With each child in a group writing the
next line of a story as paper is passed
from one player to the next, this game
is a test of your child's imagination and
encourages her to think creatively as she
builds on each story that comes her way
during the game.

How to play
Each player writes the opening lines of a story
at the top of her sheet of paper. She passes the
paper on to the next player, who reads what
the first player has written, and adds the next
sentence. The game continues like this until each
player has had a turn. On the last round, each
player must write a sentence to end the story.
The players then take it in turns to read out
their stories.

Variations
* Agree on main characters before starting
  the game, but keep each section of the
  story hidden from the other players until
  everyone has had a turn.
* Choose a theme, such as horror, comedy
  or romance.
* With just two or three players, go round
  several times before agreeing when to
  write the final sentence.

Tips for beginners
* All start with the same first line, and
  discuss what you are going to write.
* Say out loud what you are writing.
* Take dictation from other players.

Inside story

Age range 5+
Number of players One, with adult helper
What you will need A sheet of paper and a pencil; coloured pencils (optional)

Your child will be pleased if he spots all of the triangles within the triangle below, although there is a chance he will get caught out. You can increase the number of triangles and, therefore, the complexity of the game for older children.

Preparation
Copy the illustration to draw a large triangle divided into four smaller triangles.

How to play
Show the triangle to your child and ask him to count the triangles in the drawing. If he says 'four', point out that he has forgotten to count the original triangle holding all the others, so there are five in total.

Variation
* Draw a larger triangle split into more parts, or draw a square that is four squares across by four squares down (see illustration). This has 21 squares in total (see page 124).

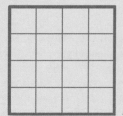

Tip for beginners
* Draw over each triangle in a different colour to emphasize how each one is made.

House builder

Age range 8+
Number of players One, with adult helper
What you will need A sheet of paper and a pencil

Can your child draw a house using one continuous line? This is a great visual trick – even if you demonstrate (with reasonable speed) your child will not be able to see how you did it. He will enjoy catching his friends out, too.

How to play
Copy the house onto your sheet of paper (see illustration, below) and ask your child to draw the shape without taking his pencil off the paper. He must use only eight lines and he may not go over the same line twice.

Variation
* There is more than one way to draw the house (see page 124). Can your child find any others?

Tip for beginners
* Omit the crossed lines in the centre of the house, which makes the house simpler to draw.

Where is my pup?

Age range 6+
Number of players One, with adult helper

This is a clever visual game for your child. In telling her a story about a missing dog, you gradually draw the face of a puppy. It is a good test of your child's visual and aural skills, and whether she can use them both at the same time. Older children can try the game out on each other.

How to play

Tell the following story to your child, copying the illustrations as you go. See how soon your child realizes that you are actually creating a picture of a dog along the way!

The story

There was once a man who lost his dog (1). He went looking for it everywhere. First he went to a lake (2). Then he searched in two dark caves (3), and climbed over a mountain (4). The poor man looked for two long (y)ears...(5). And at last, he found his beloved dog!

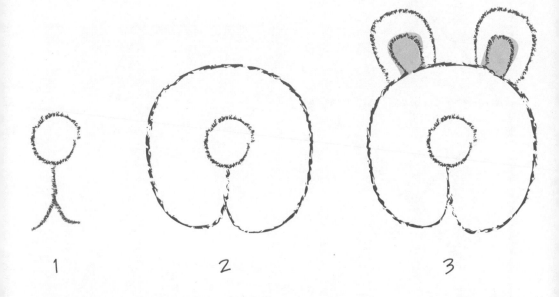

1   2   3

What you will need A sheet of paper and
a pencil

Tip for beginners
* Draw faint outlines at each stage and let
  your child draw over them as you build up
  the picture.

Variation
* Make a cat instead by drawing two pointed
  ears (he climbed over two steep hills) and
  whiskers (he searched six roads, three
  in one direction, and three the other).

4

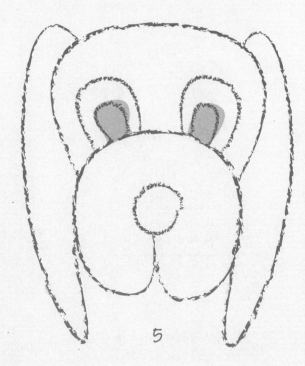

5

It takes two

Age range 9+
Number of players One, with adult helper
What you will need A sheet of paper and a pencil

See if your child can spot a deliberate error in a sentence you ask her to read out. This illusion is a good test of her eye for detail, but will only work once. When she has mastered it, she can test her friends in the same way.

Preparation
Write a simple expression within a triangle, repeating one of the words at the end of one line and the beginning of the next. A classic to try is:

I
love
Paris in
in springtime

Alternatively, you can make up your own sentences. For example:

I
had to
go to the
the doctor's

Dogs
always
chase after any
any ball you throw

How to play
Ask your child to read her triangular notice. Most newcomers to the game will not notice that one of the words has been repeated.

Tips for beginners
* Write the repeated word using a firmer pencil mark to help draw the eye.
* Keep the sentence to three short lines, such as:

I like
like cheese
in my sandwich

Variation
* Try putting in two repeated words in a longer sentence. For example:

Fish
can easily be
be caught when
you have the right
right fishing gear with you.

Age range 8+
Number of players Any number
What you will need A sheet of paper and a pencil for each player

Future fun

Does your child dream about her future? Does she wonder what life has in store for her? This game has all the answers – who she will marry, where she will live – and how many children she will have!

Preparation
Draw a large square. Along the top, write the letters MASH; down one side write four boys' names (if the player is a girl); down the other side write four countries; along the bottom ask the player to choose four numbers between 1 and 10, and write them in.

How to play
Ask the player to choose a number between 1 and 6. Starting at the M, count around the square in a clockwise direction, crossing off whichever word you land on that corresponds with the number the player chose. If she chose 5, for example, the first word you should cross off is 'Ireland'. Continue to count around the square in multiples of 5 until there is only one item left on each side of the square.

You then reveal that:
M stands for Mansion
A stands for Apartment
S stands for Shed
H stands for House

In this example, therefore, the player will marry a boy called David, live in a shed in India, and have three children – not bad going!

Variations
* Change the letters from homes to professions. For example, M for model; A for anthropologist; S for spaceman; H for holiday rep.
* Or think of new words. For example, DEAL could translate into: Driver; Engineer; Acrobat; Lawyer.

Tip for beginners
* Help your child by pointing at each category as she counts around the square, especially if she isn't yet confident about clockwise and anticlockwise.

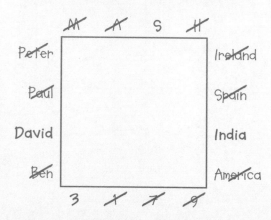

Mystic rose

Age range 8+
Number of players Any number

This drawing exercise is a great example of what you can achieve with just a pencil and paper. Your child will marvel at the beautiful shapes that emerge from nothing but straight lines, and will delight in colouring them in.

Preparation
Each child draws a large circle on a sheet of paper, using the rim of a mug or glass to make it perfect. Mark 12 dots evenly around the circumference.

How to play
Starting at any one of the dots, the child uses her ruler to draw lines joining that dot to each of the other dots in turn. Working clockwise, she repeats the process for each of the dots around the circle. A complex pattern will emerge gradually, becoming increasingly dense as more lines are drawn.

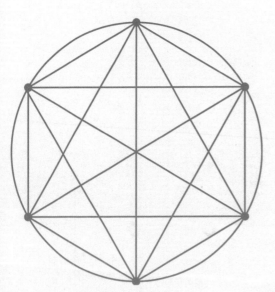
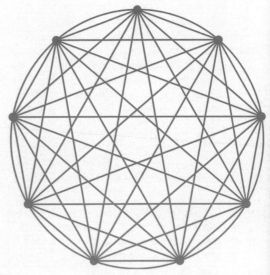

What you will need A sheet of paper and a pencil for each player; a glass or mug; a ruler for each player; coloured pencils (optional)

Tips for beginners
* Mark each of the dots with the numbers 1 to 12, like the face of a clock. This makes it easier to follow which dot is linked to which.
* Mark out only six dots if 12 makes the game too complicated.

Variations
* Mark 20 dots around the edge of the circle to make the pattern more complex.
* Colour in the intricate patterns within the whole rose.
* Try different links between the dots, for example link 1 to 3; 2 to 4; 3 to 5 and so on.

Sunshine lines

Age range 7+
Number of players Two or more
What you will need A sheet of paper and a pencil; a ruler

The radiating lines in this illustration create an optical illusion, persuading the viewer that the horizontal lines are not straight, but curved. This picture is simple enough for your child to draw himself and try out on his friends.

Tip for beginners
* Give a player the ruler to check the 'curves' for himself, if he is not convinced.

Preparation
Copy the illustration. Start by drawing a small circle in the centre of the paper, with another smaller circle within it. Draw a series of long, straight lines radiating out from the larger circle in a sunburst, but avoid drawing any that are completely vertical. Now draw in the two straight lines of identical length, above and below the circles.

Variation
* Make one of the straight lines thicker than the other. This has the effect of making the thinner line look even more curved.

How to play
Each player has to say in turn whether he thinks the horizontal lines are straight or curved. The winner is the one to guess correctly that both are straight.

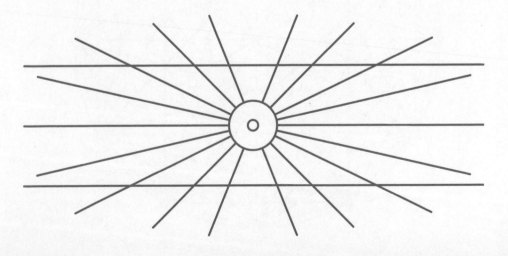

Age range 8+
Number of players Any number, with adult helper
What you will need A sheet of paper and a pencil; a ruler; scissors; a different coloured sheet of paper for each player (optional); an egg timer or stopwatch (optional)

Where will it fit?

This game is based on tessellation and is a really good test of your child's visual-spatial skills. Can he 'read' the pieces of a puzzle to see how they might fit together to make a square?

Preparation
Draw a large 16-square grid on a sheet of paper, four squares across by four squares down. Divide the square into a number of tessellating shapes – that is, shapes that interlock – using the grid squares as a guide (see illustration). Cut out the main square, then all the individual pieces. Repeat the process for each player. (You can speed this up by cutting through several sheets of paper at the same time.) If you use a different coloured sheet of paper for each player you will avoid the pieces getting mixed up.

How to play
Mix up each player's pieces of paper and see how quickly he can put them back together to recreate the original square. You can either time each player's record, or ask all the players to start at the same time and see who finishes first.

Tips for beginners
* Make a smaller square with less divisions.
* Use paper that is only coloured on one side so there is no confusion about which way up the pieces should be.

Variation
* Draw a larger square with more complicated divisions.

Which is bigger?

Age range 6+
Number of players Two or more
What you will need A sheet of paper and a pencil; a bottle top or cork

This is a straightforward optical illusion. See how long it takes your child to spot the fact that two circles are the same size, although one looks larger than the other.

Preparation

Draw two identical circles on the sheet of paper, spaced well apart and using a bottle top or cork to make sure they are the same. Copy the illustration to draw 12 smaller circles around the left-hand circle, in a petal formation. Draw fewer, larger circles around the right-hand circle.

Tip for beginners

* Help a younger player to draw her own two circles around the rim of an upturned cup. Add the extra circles around the edge so that she can see for herself how the illusion works.

Variation

* Draw several of these circle illusions on different sheets of paper, but make one of them the odd one out, in that it actually does have different sized circles. See which of the players can spot the difference when you show all of the pictures in turn.

How to play

Place the two flower pictures in front of the players, and ask each in turn which has the larger circle in its centre. It looks as if the left-hand circle is larger, so the winner is the first to realize that both circles are, in fact, identical.

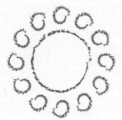

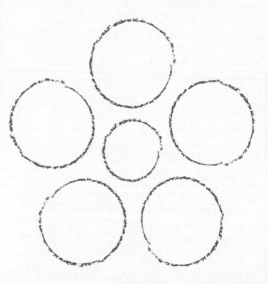

Age range 9+
Number of players Any number
What you will need A sheet of paper;
coloured pencils; scissors (optional)

Colour coded

This game is a visual tongue twister!
Your child has to read one thing but say
another and it is amazing to see just how
difficult this can be. The exercise is a test
of your child's powers of concentration.

Preparation

Write a list of colours, using appropriately
coloured pencils: for example, use a red pencil to
write the word red; a green pencil to write green;
a blue pencil to write blue; and a yellow pencil to
write yellow. Repeat the process twice more.
Now use a different coloured pencil to write
each colour name. For example, use a blue pencil
to write the word red; a red pencil to write
green; a yellow pencil to write blue; and a green
pencil to write yellow.

How to play

Each player takes a turn at reading out the
colours, but she must say which colour the word
is written in, not the word itself. So, for example,
where yellow is written in red pencil, she should
say 'red'. The other players watch carefully as the
player goes through the list – and stop her as
soon as she makes a mistake.

The winner is the player who gets furthest down
the list without getting a colour wrong.

Tips for beginners
* Use only two colours to begin with.
* Allow plenty of time for each word.

Variations
* Make the game a speed contest so that the
  players have to read through the list more
  and more quickly.
* To vary the game, cut out each of the
  colour names and rearrange them any
  number of times to make a fresh game.
* Introduce extra colours.

Switch it round

Age range 10+
Number of players One, with adult helper

This test of your child's visual skills involves using matchsticks to change the shape of a simple diagram. Many children find the game quite challenging until they have had some practice.

Preparation
Copy the illustration below (1) to create the four-square out of 12 matchsticks on a sheet of paper.

How to play
Instruct your child to make a new pattern of just three squares. He can move four of the matchsticks to make the new shape, but he has to use them all. See how few moves it takes your child to complete the task. (See solution below.)

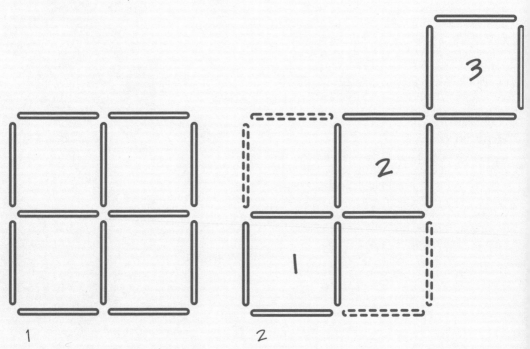

What you will need A sheet of paper; matchsticks; a pencil (optional); an eraser (optional)

3

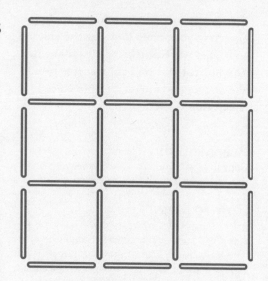

Variations

* Try a more complicated shape, using 24 matchsticks to make up a nine-square figure. Your child must remove eight matchsticks to leave only two squares. (See solution, bottom right).
* The game can also be played using a pencil and eraser.

Tip for beginners

* Mark out the solution on a piece of paper so that your child can see how to move the pieces. Use a different coloured pencil for the lines that show the solution.

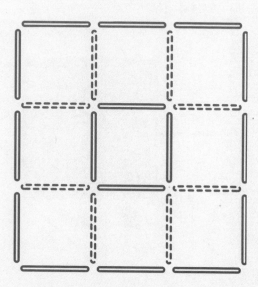

4

Which side is on top?

Age range 10+
Number of players Any number, with adult helper
What you will need A sheet of paper and a pencil

This is a great visual trick. Depending on how long your child looks at the shaded cube, she will begin to see it differently. The optical illusion confuses her mind and she will no longer be able to tell which side is shaded.

Variation

* Shade different sides of the box to see whether they can change too.

Preparation

Copy the illustration to draw a cube with one side coloured a deeper shade than the rest.

How to play

Ask the players to look carefully at the cube. At first it will seem as though the shaded side of the cube is inside the back of the cube. But stare long enough and suddenly it all changes. The shaded side is suddenly on the top right of the cube – and on the outside, at that!

Tip for beginners

* Draw the illusion twice and shade the same section in each cube differently to emphasize how the illusion works. Shade lightly for a box with a coloured back wall, and more heavily for a box with a coloured top (see illustration).

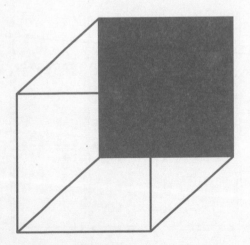
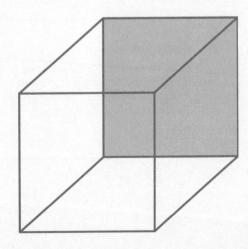

Age range 10+
Number of players One, with adult helper
What you will need A sheet of paper and
a pencil

Back to the beginning

This is a brilliant brain teaser based on mathematics. Your child chooses a number, does some simple arithmetic and ends up with the number she started with! This is one that she can try out on her friends.

How to play
Give your child the following instructions: Write down a number between 1 and 9. Multiply that number by 3. Add 1 and multiply by 3 again. Now add on the number you first thought of. Tell your child that you know she now has a two-figure number that ends in a 3. Ask her to cross off that 3 and she will be left with the number she first wrote down.

Tip for beginners
* Check on your child's maths as the trick goes along to make sure that she makes no mistakes.

5
$5 \times 3 = 15$
$15 + 1 = 16$
$16 \times 3 = 48$
$48 + 5 = 53$
5̶3̶

Variation
* Try this one: Ask your child to choose a number between 1 and 10. Add 1 and multiply by 2. Add 3 and multiply by 2 again. Subtract 10. Now ask your child to tell you her final number – and amaze her by telling her the original number (which you arrive at by dividing her final number by 4).

Talking vase

Age range 7+
Number of players One, with adult helper

This is a simple, but effective, two-way illusion. Depending on which part of the image your child focuses on, he will either see two heads facing each other or an ornate vase. With a little practice he will be able to switch between the two with each blink.

Preparation
Copy the illustration to draw two faces in profile, facing each other. Do not include any features at this point.

How to play
Ask your child if he can see two people talking to each other. Ask him to look again. This time, can he see a curved vase?

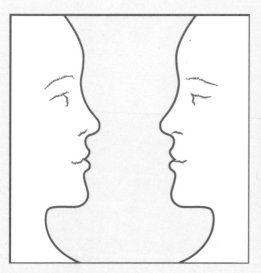

What you will need A sheet of paper and
a pencil; scissors (optional)

Tip for beginners

* Draw the same illusion twice. On one,
  add features to each of the faces to make
  it clear that they are facing each other
  (see illustration, far left). On the second
  illusion, add a top and bottom to the vase
  and draw flowers coming out of the top
  (see illustration, right). Younger players will
  enjoy colouring in the flowers, or giving
  the faces hair and features.

Variations

* Ask your child to create his own illusions.
* Fold the paper in half and draw on one half
  of the picture on the fold. Cut this out, and
  then unfold it to reveal the illusion.

Time pairs

Age range 5+
Number of players Two, with adult helper
What you will need Two sheets of paper
and a pencil; scissors

**Based on the traditional game of pairs,
this game is a very good test of your
child's memory. It uses clock faces
showing the hours of the day and will
also help your child to learn how to tell
the time.**

Preparation
Cut each sheet of paper into 12 identical
rectangles and draw a simple clock face on each
one. On the first two cards draw in the hands
showing midday. On the second two cards draw
the hands showing one o'clock. Continue until
you have two cards for each hour of the day.

How to play
Lay the cards face down on the table and ask the
first child to turn over two cards. If they tell the
same time, she can keep the cards and have
another go. If they tell different times, she returns
the cards, face down, while the second child takes
a turn. The game continues until all of the cards
have been paired. The winner is the player with
the most pairs.

Tip for beginners
* Say the hour as your child turns over the
  card and point to the number on the
  clock face.

Variation
* To make the game harder, add in some
  extra cards, first showing some half-hours,
  then some quarter-past hours, and finally
  some quarter-to hours. Remember to
  make two cards of each, so there is a pair
  of each.

Age range 6+
Number of players Any number, with adult helper
What you will need A sheet of paper and a pencil

Highest and lowest

This is an interesting game in which your child needs to put a range of numbers in the correct numerical order. The challenge lies in the fact that some of the numbers are written as figures, while others are written as words.

Variations
* If there are several children playing this game, have a race, with winners for each round and an overall 'best of three'.
* Instead of writing out the whole list, just ask them to write down the lowest number and the highest number.

Preparation
Write out three lists of five numbers that are not in numerical order, using both figures and words, and tailoring the lists to the age range of the children playing. For example:

six, 4, 1, five, 2

21, thirteen, 9, three, eleven

one hundred and one, 100, zero, 10, ninety-nine

How to play
Ask your child if she can rearrange each list so that all the numbers read in the correct numerical order. For example:

1, 2, 4, five, six

three, 9, eleven, thirteen, 21

zero, 10, ninety-nine, 100, one hundred and one

Tips for beginners
* Suggest your child converts the written numbers into figures before putting the numbers in order, so that she is doing one thing at a time.
* Remind her to watch out for the number of zeros each number has.

63 six 2 eleven

Spotty ladybirds

Age range 4+
Number of players One, with adult helper

This fun numerical game will help your child understand the difference between even and odd numbers. Played in a similar way to Time Pairs (see page 92), all your child has to do is to count the spots on the ladybirds and collect either the odd or even ones in a pile.

Preparation

Cut each sheet of paper into ten equal-sized rectangles and draw the outline of a ladybird on each one (an oval with six legs and two feelers). Colour each ladybird red and add on black spots, giving ten ladybirds an even number of spots (2, 4, 6, 8 or 10), and ten odd (1, 3, 5, 7 or 9).

How to play

Lay the cards out face down in front of your child and decide who is going to collect the even numbers and who the odd ones. Take turns to turn over a card, one at a time, and count the spots on it. If the number of spots matches what your child is collecting, he can keep it. For example, if he is collecting even numbers and turns over a ladybird with four spots on it, he keeps the card. Otherwise, the card must be turned back over. The first person to collect all ten of their cards wins.

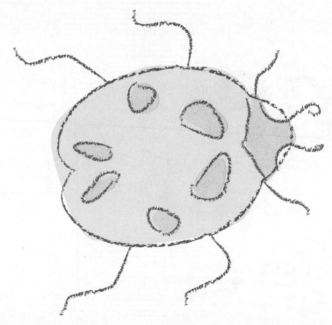

What you will need Two sheets of paper and a pencil; scissors; red and black crayons

Tips for beginners
* Write out the even and odd numbers in two rows for your child to refer to.
* For young children, lie all the cards out face up and sort them into two piles of even and odd spots together.
* Keep the number of spots small, say, no more than four on each one.

Variations
* Increase the number of spots according to your child's counting ability.
* Make caterpillars instead, with varying numbers of legs.

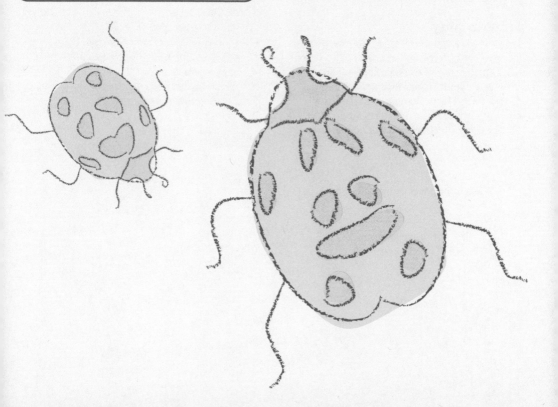

Noughts and crosses

Age range 4+
Number of players One, with adult helper
What you will need A sheet of paper;
a pencil for each player; coloured pens
(optional)

Although this game does not use numbers, it does require an understanding of symbols and basic strategy when it comes to beating an opponent. The aim of the game is to be the first to make a complete line of either noughts or crosses.

Preparation
Copy the illustration below to draw a grid of nine spaces.

How to play
Let your child choose whether she wants to be 'noughts' or 'crosses' and instruct her to draw her symbol in any of the nine spaces. Then you draw your symbol in another space. Continue to take turns like this until one person has a complete line of three of their symbol (vertically, horizontally or diagonally) and can draw a line through it.

Tips for beginners
* Diagonal lines are hardest for young kids to spot, so give your child a hint if possible.
* Use different coloured pens to make the lines even easier for little ones to spot.

Variations
* Make a larger grid of 16, 25 or 36 spaces, scoring for each run of your symbol. Score one point for a line of three, two for a line of four, and three for a line of five.
* Older children may like to play the game between themselves.

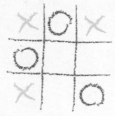

Number crossword

Age range 7+
Number of players One, with adult helper
What you will need A sheet of paper and a pencil

This game is a great test of your child's basic arithmetic. She must fill the gaps in the crossword by completing the sums. The challenge is that, in order to arrive at the answers, she must calculate each sum in reverse.

Preparation

Copy the 25-square grid – five down by five across – blacking out four squares and filling in the white squares with numbers as shown. The gaps are the squares that your child will fill in.

Show the grid to your child and ask her if she can work out what the missing numbers are.

3	+		=	4
+		+		−
3	−	2	=	
=		=		=
6	−	3	=	3

A more difficult grid might include multiplication and division symbols (see illustration, below).

3	×		=	9
×		÷		−
	+	1	=	5
=		=		=
12	÷	3	=	

Tip for beginners
* Remind players to look at symbols carefully.

Variation
* Older children can make up number crosswords of their own to try on friends.

It's a line up!

Age range 7+
Number of players Two

This game of strategy is a variation on the theme of **Noughts and Crosses** (see page 96). Each player needs to create a line of four squares with the same symbol, while preventing his opponent from doing the same.

Preparation
Draw a 42-square grid – seven across by six down (see illustration, below).

How to play
Using a different coloured pencil each, the players take turns to mark either noughts or crosses respectively in the squares. A player can only draw one mark at a time and he must build up from the bottom of the grid (imagine each column as a chute and the noughts and crosses as items dropped down the chutes). The idea is for a player to make a line of four squares of his symbol, while trying to stop his opponent from doing the same. The winner is the first to make a horizontal, vertical or diagonal line of four.

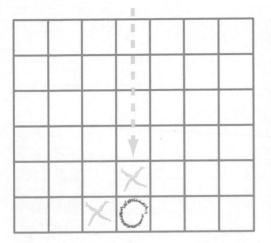

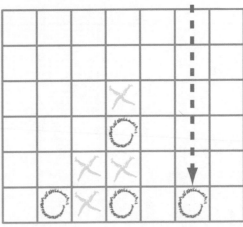

What you will need A sheet of paper and
a pencil; a coloured pencil for each player

Tips for beginners
* If you imagine that the grid is governed by
  the law of gravity it will help you to
  understand that your marks must always
  be made in the bottom-most square of
  any one column.
* Be particularly wary of an opponent
  making a diagonal line.

Variation
* Draw a larger grid for a longer game.

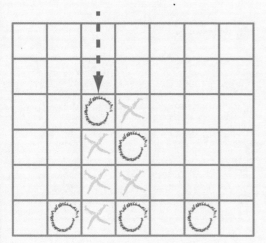
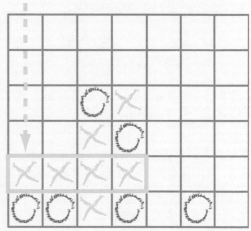

It all adds up

Age range 8+
Number of players One, with adult helper
What you will need A sheet of paper and a pencil

This is a basic number puzzle in which your child has to decode the symbols in a grid in order to produce their corresponding numbers. Use the grid to test her arithmetic and your child will be surprised to find that the numbers in any one column or row make the same total when added together.

Preparation

Draw two 25-square grids – five across by five down – and erase the bottom-right-hand-corner square on each (see illustration, below). Above the two grids, write out a set of symbols representing the numbers 1 to 5. For example, the symbols might look like this:

1 = ●   2 = *   3 = ▲
4 = ∫   5 = □

For the left-hand grid copy the illustration given below, placing the right symbol in each of 16 squares, as shown.

*	●	▲	▲	
∫	*	*	●	
●	□	*	●	
*	●	*	∫	

How to play

Give the sheet of paper to your child and ask her to fill in the empty grid, using the code at the top to swap the symbols for numbers. When she has done this, ask her to add up each row across, writing the total in the square at the end of the row. Tell her to do the same with each column and watch her amazement as each total comes to 9!

2	1	3	3	9
4	2	2	1	9
1	5	2	1	9
2	1	2	4	9
9	9	9	9	

Variation

* Make your own version where the numbers all add up to different totals, in which case you can use symbols for every figure between 1 and 9.

Tip for beginners

* Make a smaller grid with fewer numbers.

Age range 9+
Number of players Any number, with
adult helper
What you will need A sheet of paper and
a pencil for each player; an extra sheet of
paper; an egg timer or stopwatch

Guess the gaps

This exercise can pose a real test of your
child's mental agility. She has to figure
out the pattern in a given sequence of
numbers and fill in numbers where there
are gaps. You can make the sequences
more obvious for younger children.

$$3 \times 3 = 9$$

$$5 \times 4 = 20$$

$$6 \times 7 = 42$$

Preparation

Cut the extra sheet of paper into six strips
and write a sequence of numbers on each one,
omitting every other number. Here are a few
examples of sequences to try:

Consecutive numbers:
1, –, 3, –, 5, –, 7, –, 9
Alternate numbers: 2, –, 6, –, 10, –, 14
Adding 3:   1, –, 7, –, 13, –, 19, –, 25
3x table: 3, –, 9, –, 15, –, 21
4x table: –, 8, –, 16, –, 24
5x table: 5, –, 15, –, 25, –

How to play

Place a row of numbers on the table and give the
children two minutes to copy out the list and add
in the missing numbers. The players score points
according to the number of people playing. For
example, if there are three children playing, the
first person to finish gets three points, the second
two, and the third one. The winner is the player
with the highest score at the end of the game.

Variations

* Instead of having the same gap each time,
  keep adding on one more number as you
  go up. For example,
  1, (2), 4, (7), 11, (16), 22.
* Start each sequence with a higher number
  rather than with 1. For example,
  46, (48), 50, (52), 54.

Tips for beginners

* Leave fewer blanks and keep them
  towards the end of each sequence.
* Give a clue if a child gets stuck: 'Think
  of your four times table', for example.

Battleships

Age range 8+
Number of players Two

Battleships has been a favourite seek-and-destroy game for many generations. Based on a simple grid formation, the idea is to discover your opponent's fleet of ships before he finds yours.

Preparation

Each player draws two 100-square grids, ten across by ten down. He writes the letters A to J above each square across the top of each grid, and the numbers 1 to 10 beside each square down the left-hand side. Each player then 'hides' his fleet of ships in one of the grids by colouring in the squares according to the key below. The ships can run vertically or horizontally within the grid, but no two ships may touch. Each player's fleet contains: one battleship, two cruisers, three destroyers and four submarines.

Key to the fleet

Battleship = four adjacent squares in a row
Cruisers = three adjacent squares in a row
Destroyers = two adjacent squares in a row
Submarines = one separate square

Tip for beginners

* Explain clearly to the players how to read the letters and numbers across and down to name the location.

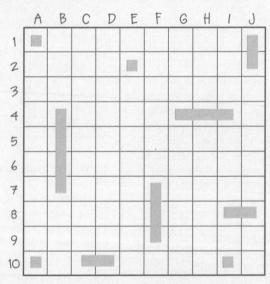

What you will need Two sheets of paper and a pencil for each player

How to play

It is important that neither player sees his opponent's grids at any point during the game. The idea is that each player has to guess where his opponent has hidden his fleet. Players take it in turns to ask about specific locations, quoting the grid reference for a particular square each time. For example, the first player may say 'B2'. If the square is empty, his opponent answers 'miss'; if he does have a ship there, he answers 'hit', but does not reveal the type of ship that has been hit. The first player puts a circle in the corresponding square of his empty grid for a miss, or a cross for a hit. A player who scores a hit may guess another square immediately. Otherwise it is his opponent's turn to guess. Play continues in this way until a whole ship for either player is discovered, at which point the person whose ship

Variation

* Invent your own alternatives for ships, such as vehicles, aliens, or monsters (for example, one Megamonster, two Maximonsters, three Minimonsters and four Micromonsters).

it is shouts 'sunk!'. Since no two ships are allowed to touch, all of the squares around the sunk ship can be filled in with circles for water. The winner is the first person to discover his opponent's entire fleet of ships.

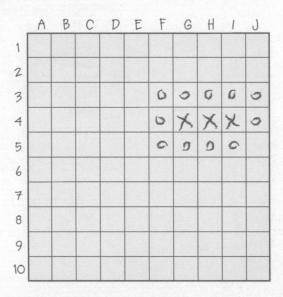

Race track

Age range 4+
Number of players Two or more, with adult helper
What you will need A sheet of paper and a pencil; a different coloured counter for each player; a die

This is a fun first-past-the-post board game. Instead of relying simply on the luck of the die to produce a winner, this game has bonuses and forfeits along the way to make it more of a challenge.

Preparation

Draw a curving track of two parallel lines on a large sheet of paper. Divide the track into segments and number them consecutively. Write 'start' next to the first segment and 'finish' next to the last one. Write in a few 'bonuses' in a couple of the remaining segments, say, 'Move on two places', 'Have an extra go' or 'Move your opponent back one space'. Write in some forfeits as well. 'Move back one', 'Miss a turn', or 'Move your opponent forward one', for example.

How to play

Place a counter for each player on the starting line. The players take turns to throw the die, moving their counters forward by the same number of segments as they throw. Depending on which segment each player lands on, she may have to play a forfeit or a bonus, or simply wait for her next turn. A player who throws a 6 may have another go. The first person to the finishing line is the winner.

Variations

* Personalize the race track to suit the interests of the children. For instance it could be a horse, car or motorbike race track; or bunnies finding their way home to their burrow.
* Try to match the bonuses and forfeits to the theme – for example, 'Wheel comes off. Miss a go'.

Tip for beginners
* Keep the number of segments reasonably low – around 20 should be fine.

Age range 7+
Number of players Two or more, with a caller
What you will need A sheet of paper and a pencil for each player; two dice

Bingo dice

In this game of bingo, the numbers are determined by the roll of two dice. The element of competition will appeal to your child and you will be able to sense the tension mounting as the game nears the end. Who will be the first to get a **Full House?**

Preparation
Each player writes a list of numbers from 1 to 12. Beside this list, the player writes a list of numbers from 12 down to 1 (see illustration, below).

How to play
The caller throws the dice and calls out the two numbers rolled. Each player can strike through the two numbers on her score sheet, or can add the two numbers together to strike through the resulting larger number.

For example, if the caller says '2 and 4', a player can either strike through a 2 and a 4 from her sheet, or through a 6 alone. A 6 and 3 called could mean crossing through a 6 and a 3, or a 9 alone. The winner is the first player to cross through all 24 numbers.

1	12
2	11
3	10
4	9
5	8
6	7
7	6
8	5
9	4
10	3
11	2
12	1

Tip for beginners
* Mark out a sheet of paper with nine squares in it (three rows of three squares), each containing a random number from 1 to 6, and repeating whichever numbers you like. Then play as above, using one die only.

Variation
* Create a bingo card with 9, 16, 25, 36 or more squares, with each square containing a number from 1 to 12 chosen at random, repeating numbers of choice.

Link the wagons

Age range 4+
Number of players One, with adult helper

This fun game will help your child to develop his numerical skills – all he has to do is arrange a series of numbered train wagons in the correct order behind the engine.

Preparation

Draw the outline of a train engine at the top of the sheet of paper, followed by ten simple wagons (rectangles with three wheels at the bottom). In each wagon write a number, from 1 to 10. Cut out the engine and each of the wagons.

How to play

Jumble the wagons up and, passing the engine to your child, tell him that the engine has got its wagons in a muddle and needs him to help put them in the right order again. Instruct your child to arrange the wagons in a line behind the engine, so that they run in the correct numerical order. When he has finished, he can colour in the engine and wagons.

Variations

* Make the game more difficult for an older child by having a few wagons with wrong numbers on them, such as 17 or 20.
* Try the game with other objects in a line, such as numbered beads on a necklace, footballers in a team, or baby ducks following a mother duck.

Tips for beginners

* Start with just five wagons.
* Write the numbers out in the correct order on a separate piece of paper.

What you will need A sheet of paper and
a pencil; scissors; coloured crayons (optional)

Stretch it

Age range 4+
Number of players Any number, with adult helper
What you will need Four sheets of paper and a pencil for each player; a die

Children love playing this game, tumbling over each other as they twist and bend to position themselves. It is a game that needs adult supervision: not only will you need to throw the die for the children, but you should also make sure the children do not slip about too much on the sheets of paper.

Variation
* If there are no available number sheets of paper left, you can throw the die again instead of the player having to try sharing a sheet of paper with someone else.

Preparation
Give each child four sheets of paper and ask her to write down four numbers between 1 and 6 on the separate pieces. Scatter the papers across the floor, number side up.

How to play
Throw the die for each player in turn. Whatever number you roll, that player must put her right foot on a sheet of paper with the same number. Play continues until all players have a right foot on a number. In the next round each of the players places her left foot on a sheet of paper with each roll of the die. In the third round, each player puts her the right hand on a sheet of paper, and in the fourth round she places her left hand on a sheet of paper. Anyone who falls over during the game is out.

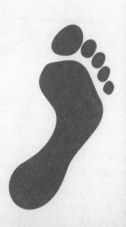

Tips for beginners
* Keep the pieces of paper close together.
* Play where each player simply jumps onto the right number with each roll of the die.

Magic square

Age range 10+
Number of players One, with adult helper
What you will need A sheet of paper and
a pencil

Find out what your child makes of this
challenging puzzle. It is a really good test
of her mental arithmetic, although she
can also find the solution through trial
and error. Either way, she will enjoy
testing her friends with the puzzle once
she has mastered it herself.

1 2 3 4 5 6 7 8 9

Preparation
Draw a nine-square grid, three squares down by
three squares across, with the numbers 1 to 9
written in a row above it.

How to play
Instruct your child to put one number from 1 to
9 in each of the squares (with no repetitions) so
that each horizontal, vertical and diagonal row
adds up to 15. See how long it takes her to work
it out! (See page 124 for the solution.)

Tip for beginners
* Enter the figure for the centre square, or
  write in an entire column, before your
  child begins.

Variation
* Once your child has completed the puzzle,
  ask her to double all the numbers in it and
  see what happens when she adds up all the
  lines and diagonals now. (They should all
  add up to 30.)

Dot-to-dot letters

Age range 4+
Number of players One, with adult helper
What you will need A sheet of paper and a pencil; an eraser

In this game of dot to dot, your child needs to move from one letter of the alphabet to the next in order to draw a picture. This is a very effective way of helping him to learn the alphabet.

Preparation
Lightly draw a picture outline of, say, a house, boat or teddy on the sheet of paper. Pick out 26 places to make a dot on the outline of the image, and then erase the faint line drawing. Write a letter of the alphabet beside each dot, working your way around the picture alphabetically, until you come back to the beginning.

How to play
Ask your child to make the picture by drawing a line from one letter of the alphabet to the next, starting at A and finishing at Z.

Variations
* Traditionally this game is played with numbers. Simply write the figures 1 to 26 instead of the letters A to Z.
* If your child has a reasonably long name, such as Christopher, and knows how to spell it, try connecting the letters of his name instead of the those of the alphabet.

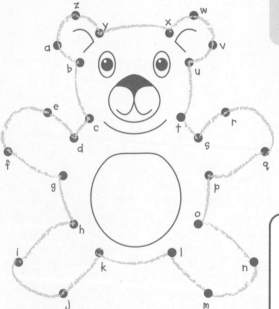

Tip for beginners
* It may help to print out the alphabet in a straight line above the picture.

Find the letters

Age range 5+
Number of players One, with adult helper
What you will need A sheet of paper and
a pencil; a felt-tipped pen

This game works in a similar way to
Word Search (see page 24) except that,
in this case, your child needs to find the
individual letters of a word in a grid. It is
a good test of his visual alertness.

Preparation
Write a word at the top of the sheet of paper.
Now write the letters of that word anywhere on
the page, at random, and 'hide' them by writing
additional, different, letters all around.

How to play
Show your child the word at the top of the page,
say elephant and ask him if he can find the letters
of that word hidden in the letter jumble below.
Each time he finds a letter he can circle it with
a brightly coloured felt-tipped pen and write it
under the word at the top of the page.

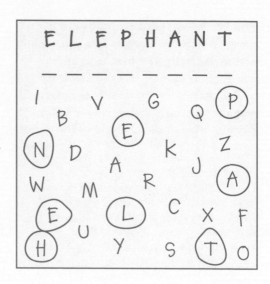

Variations
* To make the game harder, hide two or
  three words in the letter jumble.
* To make the game harder still, leave out
  one letter of the word from the letter
  jumble and ask your child if he can find
  which letter is missing.

Tip for beginners
* Very young children will find this game
  easier if you pick out the letters of the
  word in a particular colour.

Alphabet sentences

Age range 8+
Number of players Any number
What you will need A sheet of paper and a pencil

This is a game that gets harder as it progresses and will really test your child's verbal dexterity. The idea is to add a word to a sentence, where each word begins with a consecutive letter of the alphabet. There is always a very funny story to read out at the end of the game.

How to play

The first player starts writing a 'story' by putting down a word that begins with the letter 'a'. She could either use the article A, or find another word that begins with 'a', such as Alfred, Annie, armadillos, arms or angry. She then passes the paper to her left for the next person to write a word that begins with the letter 'b'. The paper moves to the left again and the third player writes a word that starts with 'c'. Play continues until the players have worked through the entire alphabet to make a reasonably coherent sentence.

Sample sentence

The type of sentence made could end up reading something like this:

Annie beheld Carol Drake eating four giant heavy iced jellied kippers, lips munching noisily, outside Peter's quarters round Swindon telling us very wittily, 'X-ray your zoo!'.

Variations

* Try a shorter version by opting for every other letter of the alphabet, for example, a, c, e, g, i, k ...; or b, d, f, h, j ...
* Make the game harder by telling everyone the 'story' must be on a particular theme, such as rock-climbing or disco dancing.
* Try making as long a sentence as possible using the same initial letter for every word of a sentence – for example, Bertie Bunny built bridges by breaking boulders.

Tip for beginners

* Improvise for the letter 'x' by allowing excite, exit or exist, or drop it altogether.

Age range 6+
Number of players One, with adult helper
What you will need A sheet of paper and a pencil; an extra sheet of paper; scissors; an egg timer or stopwatch

Missing letters

By showing familiar words to your child, but with certain letters missing, you are testing both her memory and her early spelling skills. This is a game you can play as your child's vocabulary increases, simply by using longer and more complicated words.

Preparation

Think of 20 words that you know your child can read. Write the words out, using large letters, on the extra sheet of paper, leaving enough room for you to cut each one out. As you write the words, replace the vowels with dashes. For example, if you had chosen 'dog', 'garden', 'book' and 'seaside', your cards would read: D_G, G_RD_N, B__K and S__S_D_. Also make some tiny cards with a single vowel written on each one (A, E, I, O and U), which can be placed over the dashes in your chosen words.

How to play

Place the vowel cards face up on the table. Then shuffle the 20 word cards, place them face down on the table and ask your child to pick one. She then has one minute to work out what the missing letters might be, placing the vowel cards over the dashes to fill the gaps. You may find that she can make a different word to the one you intended. For instance, instead of DOG she might come up with DIG. This is perfectly acceptable. If she completes a word within the minute she keeps the card; if she does not, you keep the card. At the end of the game count up the cards your child has managed to collect.

Variations
* Try removing five consonants instead, such as H, R, M, S and F. So 'car', 'barn' and 'time' would be CA_, BA_N and TI_E.
* Try removing just the initial letters.

Tips for beginners
* Show your child how to experiment with letter combinations by placing the small vowel cards over the dashes to see if she can make a word.
* Use words with only one vowel missing.
* Increase the time limit.

Take away one

Age range 7+
Number of players One, with adult helper
What you will need A sheet of paper and a pencil

In this game your child has to study a word and see if, by taking away one letter, he can make a new word. Keep the words short until your child has a good understanding of how to play, then encourage him to come up with examples of his own.

Preparation

Think of a list of 10 to 20 short words at random. For example, your list might include: 'house', 'task', 'chair', 'lamp', 'break' and 'shape'.

How to play

Write out one word at a time and, together with your child, see if you can take away one letter and make a new word. Explain that it may be necessary to jumble up the letters that remain to make your new word.

Sample words

House – remove U to make Hose

Task – remove T to make Ask

Chair – remove C to make Hair

Lamp – remove L, jumble up the letters and make Map

Break – remove E, jumble up the letters and make Bark

Shape – remove H, jumble up the letters and make Peas

Variations

* Remove two letters – for example, ELBOW could lose E and L and become BOW, or CIGAR could lose I and G and become CAR.
* Add a letter to make a new word – for example RAIN could become TRAIN, or MALL become SMALL.

Tip for beginners

* Draw a picture for each of the words and talk through the images first with your child. Once he knows what the two words are, he can work backwards to work out which letter to lose.

Hidden animals

Age range 7+
Number of players One, with adult helper
What you will need A sheet of paper and a pencil

This game is based on using anagrams to disguise words. The idea is to combine the jumbled letters of two words and ask your child to see if he can unscramble them. It is quite a challenge, and your child will benefit from a clue.

Preparation
Think of ten pairs of animals and write them down, mixing up their letters, to produce one new word. For example, dog and cat could become dcogat, lion and tiger could become ltiiogner, and elephant and giraffe could become eglierapfhfaent.

How to play
Show the ten mixed-up animal combinations to your child and ask him if he can rearrange the letters on the sheet of paper to find 20 lost animals. Explain that there are two lost animals in each combination. He can write his answers alongside the original mixed-up words.

Variations
* Try this game with other combinations, such as objects that go together (brush/comb, hat/coat, knife/fork), food combinations (bacon/eggs, sausages/mash, fish/chips, strawberries/cream), well-known expressions (hot/bothered, done/dusted, ready/waiting), or opposites (happy/sad, hot/cold, over/under).
* Mix up the letters randomly, but underline the initial letter of each word.

Tips for beginners
* Avoid using animal names that are long.
* Keep the letters in the same order as they appear in the original words.

Unscramble the letters

Age range 7+
Number of players Any number, with adult helper
What you will need A sheet of paper and a pencil for each player; an egg timer or stopwatch (optional)

Give your child a series of anagrams to see if she can work out what you have written. The letters of the chosen words are rewritten in alphabetical order, and each list of words shares the same theme, so this should not be too difficult.

Preparation

Choose a few themes, such as girls' names, boys' names, flowers, fruit, trees, vegetables or the names of the planets, and think of a list of between five to ten words for each theme. Then rearrange the letters of each word in alphabetical order and write a new list on a sheet of paper with the theme title at the top. Copy the list for each player in the game.

Example of play

(Note that the answers are for reference only)

Vegetables

Acorrt (carrot)

Aooptt (potato)

Aabbceg (cabbage)

Eekls (leeks)

Abens (beans)

Aeps (peas)

How to play

Give a list of rearranged words to each child and ask who can discover what all the different vegetables are by unscrambling the letters and putting them back in the right order. You can impose a time limit if you wish. When everyone has finished go through the lists to check the words are correct, and then bring out a new list.

Variations

* As players become more skilled, up the stakes by choosing harder themes, longer words, or more of them.
* The words need not always be nouns — try verbs as well. For example, your theme could be exercising and your words could be run, jump, skip, hop, kick and swim.

Tips for beginners

* Keep the words short.
* Play in teams.
* Younger children will find this more fun if you turn it into a 'story'. For instance, you could tell them that Mary-Lou loved vegetables and ate lots every day — can your child find out just how many different vegetables she ate for lunch yesterday?

Spelling bee

Age range 7+
Number of players Any number, with adult helper
What you will need A sheet of paper and a pencil for each team of players

Each child in a team takes a turn to spell a word correctly. The pressure is on, as she risks offering the chance of a bonus point to the opposition if she spells it wrongly.

Tips for beginners
* Keep the words simple.
* Allow plenty of time.
* Remind children of tricky letters, such as the silent 'k' in 'knight' and the 'f' sound of 'ph' in 'photo'.

Variations
* Play this with your child on her own, giving her one word to spell at a time.
* Try spelling easy words backwards.

Preparation
Draw up a list of some 50 or so words that you know the players can spell.

How to play
Divide the players into two teams: A and B (or some fun name of their choice, such as Bugs and Beetles). Read out a word from your list for the first player of Team A to write down on her team's sheet of paper. When she has written it, she passes the paper to the next player, who reads out the letters. If the word is spelt correctly, Team A scores one point. If it is spelt incorrectly, Team B has a chance to spell the same word for a bonus point. Play returns to the next player on Team A, who has to try to spell a new word in the same way. When each player in Team A has taken a turn, play passes to Team B. This time Team A can score bonus points for correctly spelling the words that Team B gets wrong. When both teams have finished – that is, everyone has had a go, all the points are added up to see which team has scored the most.

Beat the boat

Age range 8+
Number of players Two
What you will need A sheet of paper and a pencil for each player

This is a modern variation of the game known as 'Hangman'. The idea is to guess an opponent's mystery word before he manages to draw a boat and sail away. There are ten chances for guessing, so children need to choose their letters very wisely.

How to play

The first player thinks of a word and draws a dash on his sheet of paper for each letter of that word. The second player starts play by guessing a letter that might be in the mystery word. If he guesses correctly, the letter is written over the corresponding dash. If the letter is not in the mystery word, it is written elsewhere on the page and the first line (the base) of the boat is drawn.

Variation

* Play a double-action game where both players choose a word and guess each other's letters simultaneously. Players should choose words of the same length, and the winner is the first player to guess his opponent's word.

Play continues like this until either the word is guessed and all the letters are filled in correctly, or the boat is drawn with a wave underneath – which means it has sailed away. To draw the boat takes ten moves (see illustration, below left).

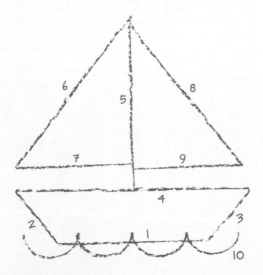

Tips for beginners

* Younger children will need very simple words that they can read easily.
* If a child is struggling, fill in the first letter of the word for him, or give a clue.

Age range 9+
Number of players Any number, with adult helper
What you will need A sheet of paper and a pencil; magnetic letters (optional)

Add a letter

In this game your child has to make a new word by adding a single letter to the word that comes before it. This is quite a challenge, so it makes sense to start with easy words to begin with, and to help your child grasp the rules of the game.

Tips for beginners
* Score one point for every word made.
* Use magnetic letters so your child can experiment with different letters.

How to play
Start the game by writing a short word at the top of a sheet of paper. You need to think carefully what that word might be to make sure that it will work for the game. Ask the first player to add one letter to make a new word and to write the new word under the old one, lining up the matching letters. Play passes to the next player who adds another letter and so on, until no further words can be made. If you get beyond five letters you are doing very well, and the person who makes the last word scores one point.

Example of play

PLAN
PLANE
PLANET
PLANETS

Variations
* An alternative method of scoring would be for the last person making a word to score a point for all previous words!
* You can also make new words from old by providing an 'inner' word and asking your child to add extra letters to either end. For example, 'add a letter to each end of "at" to make a word that means something you find in the middle of a fence' (gate); or 'add two letters to the end of "fir" to make something that comes at the beginning' (first).

Word swaps

Age range 9+
Number of players One, with adult helper
What you will need A sheet of paper and a pencil

This game is similar to Add a Letter (see page 119). Instead of adding a letter to make a new word, however, in this game your child needs to change a letter to make a new word. This is a considerable test of her verbal dexterity.

Variation
* Try the game with two four-letter words, for example:

| COLD |
| COLT |
| COAT |
| BOAT |
| BEAT |
| HEAT |

How to play
Choose two three-letter words, then see if your child can change one into the other by altering a single letter of the word at a time, making a new word each time.

Example of play
To change 'cup' into 'hat':

| CUP |
| CAP |
| CAT |
| HAT |

Tip for beginners
* Prepare the words ahead and give your child a few clues for each change. For example, to change LANE into PATH, you could say, 'The first word is a sheet of glass (PANE), the second word is something you might spread on toast (PATE), and then you're almost there!'

Age range 10+
Number of players Any number
What you will need A sheet of paper and
a pencil

Link a line

The idea of this game is for your child to make a chain of words in which each one starts with the last letter of the word before it. The game tests your child's vocabulary, as each word must also fit in with a given theme.

Annabel
Lucy
Yvonne
Elizabeth
Hannah
Hazel
Leanne
Evelyn
Nadine
Emma
Ashling
Gretta...

How to play
The first player chooses a theme, say girls' names, and writes down the first word, for example ANNABEL. That person then passes the paper to the next player, who has to find a name that begins with the last letter, in this case 'L', so LUCY. The paper is handed on again and the next person must write a name beginning with 'Y', such as YVONNE. The words cannot be repeated during the game, and play continues until players can no longer think of words to add.

Tip for beginners
* Practise by showing your child how to link any word in this way without a theme, so she does not have to think of two things at once. For instance HOUSE, EGG, GREEN and NET.

Variation
* Some themes are harder to find linking words for than others, so choose them carefully. Suggestions include: foods, animals, countries or towns.

Grid challenge

Age range 8+
Number of players Any number, with adult helper
What you will need A sheet of paper and a pencil for each player; a red felt-tipped pen; an egg timer or stopwatch

This game is great fun, and sets your child the challenge of making words from a given set of letters. Children enjoy competing with each other to see who can make the most words, and they are always amazed at how many words can be made using just nine letters.

Preparation
Draw a large nine-square grid, three squares across by three squares down. Write a vowel (a, e, i, o or u) in the middle square using a red felt-tipped pen. Add more letters at random in the other squares, including at least two extra vowels.

S	H	P
T	A	E
N	R	I

How to play
Explain that each player needs to write down as many words as he can think of using the letters in the grid. Each word can be of two or more letters and must include the red vowel in the centre. Players can use each letter only once in a word. Set a time limit of, say, five or ten minutes. At the end of this time compare all the words. You can either score a point for each word, with extra points for words of five letters or more, or score points only for those words that no other players have written down.

an	hair	star
as	pain	rain
at	sane	sari
ape	past	shape
ate	pair	satin
ash	part	paste
air	rash	haste
ant	nape	stair
hat	near	stare
eat	pear	heart...

Tips for beginners
* Choose letters carefully, with at least one 'e' and 'a', and a selection of letters that go together, such as 'th', 'ing', 'st' and 'wh'.
* Give a few prompts, such as 'Oh look, there's "in". If you put that "t" or "b" in front of "in" would you get another word?'

Variations
* Allow any letter in the grid to be used more than once when making a word.
* Omit the rule that the red vowel has to appear in each word.

Letter ladders

Age range 11
Number of players One
What you will need A sheet of paper and a pencil

This is quite a difficult game, requiring your child to work with a visual puzzle as well as a verbal one. Once he gets the idea, he will enjoy setting himself the greater challenge of using longer words, and testing his friends with the game.

How to play

Choose a four-letter word, such as 'gift', 'farm', 'arch' or 'word', and follow the illustration to write the word twice vertically on your sheet of paper – once with the letters in the correct order and once running backwards (1). Now try to make new words by building letter 'steps' of the same length between the two rows of letters. For example, if you had chosen the word 'term', your steps might look something like this (2):

Tip for beginners

* This is a difficult game, so be prepared to offer lots of help at the beginning.

Variations

* Use five- or six-letter starter words.
* Try making the 'steps' of three or four letters, although this is hard.

1
```
T          M

E          R

R          E

M          T
```

2
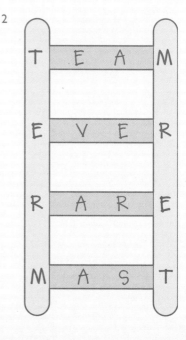
```
T  E  A  M

E  V  E  R

R  A  R  E

M  A  S  T
```

Solutions
to puzzles

Page 57
Busy hexagon
There are an amazing 114 triangles.

Page 74
Inside story

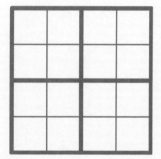

Page 75
House builder

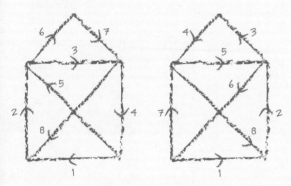

Page 97
Number crossword

3	×	3	=	9
×		÷		–
4	+	1	=	5
=		=		=
12	÷	3	=	4

3	+	1	=	4
+		+		–
3	–	2	=	1
=		=		=
6	–	3	=	3

Page 109
Magic square

2	9	4
7	5	3
6	1	8

Index by age range

Index

Acknowledgements

Executive Editor: Jane McIntosh
Editor: Leanne Bryan
Executive Art Editor: Karen Sawyer
Designer: Peter Gerrish
Illustrator: Peter Liddiard
Production Controller: Nigel Reed